In the Light of
THE WORD

In the Light of
THE WORD

Sen Koshy

2022

In the Light of the Word - Published by the Indian Society for Promoting Christian Knowledge (ISPCK), Post Box 1585, 1654, Madarsa Road, Kashmere Gate, Delhi-110006,

Online Order: http://ispck.org.in/book.php

Also available on amazon.in

ISBN: 978-93-90569-42-7

Laser typeset by

ISPCK, Post Box 1585, 1654, Madarsa Road, Kashmere Gate, Delhi-110006
• *Tel:* 23866323/22

e-mail: ashish@ispck.org.in • ella@ispck.org.in
website: www.ispck.org.in

This book is dedicated to the fond memories
of my grandfather late K. Cherian Vaidyan
and my father late C.Koshy Vaidyan
who had guided and encouraged me in my spiritual life
and their steadfastness in faith had been
an inspiration in my ministry and my life.

Contents

Acknowledgements

Praise be to Lord for enabling me to write this book giving me right thoughts, wisdom and health. 'It is good for me that I have been afflicted, that I might learn thy statutes' (Psalms 119:71). This was my situation during these years.

I acknowledge the support and help I received from my friends, well-wishers and family in my attempt. Among them to mention particularly may I name Rev. Dr. Thomas Varghese who wrote the foreword for this book and Mrs. Lalitha for her suggestions.

Many thanks to Mr. V.C. Mathew for his suggestions and encouragements in writing articles. My son Sobhith and son-in-law Jerin helped by proof reading the manuscript and I express my gratitude to them. My wife Sisy daughter Subha and daughter-in-law Mamatha deserve thanks for typing, encouraging, supporting, suggesting corrections and providing materials for expansion of subjects during the course of writing the articles in this book. My mother Chinnamma deserves love and gratitude for bringing me up in Christian discipline and values. My granddaughters Serene, Rowene and Leana even though little children they are encouraged spiritually as they came to know that I am doing a spiritual work. Let this book be an eye opener to them also when they grow up.

Praise be to our God the father, Lord Jesus Christ the son, and the Holy Spirit.

Sen Koshy

Foreword

It gives me immense joy to write foreword for the book 'In the light of the word'. I am associated with Sen Koshy and his family since 1985. Along with his work after retirement he has published many articles in Christian magazines. His personal experiences with God the Almighty and the challenges due to illness, he had experienced, Sen spent much of his time at His feet 'In the light of the word' to write this book. He has explained in detail about faith, how to worship the Lord in truth and spirit, God's grace, salvation, Christian marriage, baptism and how to be assured about eternity. I must say that he has done justice to all subjects in a simplified manner.

I congratulate Sen, on this delightful attempt to publish a book and wish him all success in future endeavors.

Rev Dr Thomas Varghese
Presbyter and Author

Preface

In the light of the word is inspired to be written in the context of the Christendom diverting from the life and teachings of Jesus Christ and churches deviating from the responsibility of teaching the Gospel in truth and spirit. Many of my friends and readers of my articles published in our church magazine suggested me to enlighten upon various basic doctrines of the Bible. But I do not endeavor it because I am not a theologian as Amos said it. But I write these articles on the basis of what the spirit of God revealed to me while studying the Bible. Most Christians do not venture or aspire to learn The Bible and so, the ignorance of the church goers is capitalized by the church leaders.

Many of the churches accept seven rituals as sacraments vital for living a faithful Christian life, whereas certain other churches have only two viz: Baptism and Eucharist. Sacraments are considered as the means of receiving divine grace if it is divinely ordained. But it seems that most of them are not so. It is observed that there is no uniformity in concept or commission of any of the sacraments among churches. That makes any reasonable person to ponder for a moment whether these rites are Christ ordained, if so, why there is no clarity in the concept or its observance. My humble opinion is that the Bible shall not be interpreted as per one's self-will and whims, without observing the hermeneutics of interpretation, only to create churches and church practices. What matters is the Church envisaged by Jesus which shall be His bride. The identity of the members of His church is - "And they, continuing daily with one accord in the temple, and breaking bread from house to house, did eat their meat with gladness and singleness of heart, praising God and having favor with all the people. And the Lord added to the church daily such as should be saved" (Acts 2:46-47)

Salvation by grace through faith in the sacrifice of Jesus Christ, for the atonement of sin, is the fundamental Christian concept and its wholehearted acceptance and open witnessing is the basis for becoming the children of God and a citizen of heavenly Kingdom. Other than this what are the divine blessings we get through the so-called sacraments, I don't know. As per the New Testament the hope of a Christian is to enter the marriage feast of the Lamb of God through faith. So, Christian faith shall be understood in the right way which I try to bring out through the first chapter.

Nowadays we see many new churches spurting out differing from other traditional churches in the manner of worship. Worship in truth and spirit we see highlighted in the Bible on various occasions by Jesus and Apostles. I made an attempt to illustrate the modes of worship through the article on worship.

Worldly prosperity is not seen listed as a blessing from God. But it was the promises given to Israel as a nation. OT is only the shadow of things that are to happen in the NT period and for people redeemed by the precious blood of Jesus Christ. St. Paul unambiguously states that we must suffer with Jesus Christ to become partakers for his resurrection. The glory that is to be revealed, is the hope of a believer and the present sufferings are not worth comparing with it (Romans 8:18). Jesus said that he will make us sit along with him where he is seated, with the only condition of abiding in him while in this world. No sacraments are prescribed. This conviction prompted me to scribble in brief my opinion on the subject of Grace. Here I tried to equate grace with salvation.

An area of confusion among Christians is the teachings on eternity. I have tried to enlarge on the concept of eternity as I could discern from the Bible.

We usually consider the word Redemption and Salvation on equal footing. I have tried in this book to illustrate that redemption is the first step towards salvation which culminates in resurrection. It is the goal of the believer. In between the Christian life is a process of getting sanctified each day leading to perfection.

It is common to many spiritual leaders to assume that they are infallible. As the scribes and priests of the Jews we see many Christians among church leaders and believers of any time claiming to be more loyal to God than all others. Also, among believers, without exclusion, we too try to justify ourselves on our words and deeds. Before we claim to be righteous it is imminent that we have an awareness of ourselves in the light of the word of God.

An article on marriage is included in this collection in the context of exceeding marriage failures among Christians. I thought it proper to write on this subject in view of Christian faith figuring Jesus Christ as the bridegroom and church as the bride.

Baptism is one of the main subjects still profoundly and pervasively talked about without coming to a consensus. Different churches follow different forms according to the conviction of each. I could not find any conclusive evidence for the ritual of baptism to be accepted as a sacrament in the Bible. Even sacraments are manmade, and salvation is the gift of God, that is what matters for a believer.

Many more subjects are of concern to be dealt with in the present Christian scenario. Through this small book I am trying to provoke the thoughts of believers young and old and to have a soul searching to know whether they are in faith; So that we lead a Christian life purely based on the Word of God. May the spirit of God work in the readers through this book, I pray.

Sen Koshy

1

The Scarlet Thread of Salvation

The term scarlet thread of salvation is used by Christian authors and theologians to represent the blood of atonement from the beginning to the end of human history which is the core theme of the Bible. The blood was first shed when Adam confessed of his nakedness and shame and fear to confront God his Creator. The eternal glory and honor of God with which they were crowned was lost when -

"Greedily she engorged without restraint,
And knew not eating death;" John Milton (Paradise lost)

It could be understood that Adam and Eve were guilty, having eaten the forbidden fruit, even before he is called by God as usual. They hid from the sight of God. (Genesis 3:7-10). Their self-remedy to solve the problem did not workout. God had to kill an innocent animal to dress them up. First time the blood that represents life fell on the earth. The majestic clothing of glory, when removed, they felt naked. The animal skin is also perishable and temporary in nature.

Sin an Intruder

It was revealed to the man that sacrificing an animal was necessary to stand before God without the feel of shame or guilt due to sin whenever they found themselves not up to the mark or standard desired by God. Sacrifice became the divine law in their conscience for humans to cover-up sin. Subsequently the custom which was already designed by God, He postulated as the Law for Israelites. 'For the life of the flesh is in the blood; and I have given it to you upon the altar to make atonement for your souls; for it is the blood that makes atonement for the soul'. (Leviticus17:11). The practice of offering sacrifices as atonement, typically foreshadowing the coming of Jesus, apparently was a human requirement from the very commencement of history. Abel, son of Adam and Eve, brought the 'firstlings of his flock and the fat thereof' (Genesis 4:4). The offering must have been killed, otherwise he could not have presented the fat, which was the best part. Moreover, we are told that "righteous Abel" (so designated by Jesus [Matthew 23:35]) offered his sacrifice "by faith" (Hebrews 11:4). He did it from his innate conscience. When Noah departed from the ark after the waters of the flood subsided, he built an altar and offered sacrifices of every clean animal and bird, and Jehovah was pleased with his offering (Genesis 8:20-21). What compelled him to do that? His conscience! As one scholar noted: "According to Romans 2:14-15 conscience is innate and universal. It is not the product of environment, training, habit, race impression, or education, though it is influenced by all these factors" (Rehwinkel 1999, 136). The ancient Gentiles, therefore, were not judged by the same rule as the Jews, but they were not void of law and culpability, they were and will be judged according to their conscience. The conscience is a part of the human package, and it demonstrates a moral chasm between men and women and other biological creatures of our planet (Genesis 1:26-27)".

From the very beginning man was aware of sins and that appeasing God was necessary if they sinned. And, animal sacrifice was the way for appeasing God. There was no approved code of conduct for people. Their conscience dictated what is wrong and what is right. God interfered with people often directly to correct them with punishments. Sacrifices for forgiveness from God and recompense for damages caused to others became a practice among them. Sin was not defined till the formulation of Mosaic laws. Since the breath of God was in man, divine nature could be in their conscience in the first place. Satan being an intruder he could not enter the spirit that God breathed in man unless he is given access into the heart. Adamic sin of disobedience and the consequent deprivation from the presence of God could have been retold to generations and that could have created the awareness of God and a good conscience in the minds of generations, Also the works of God revealed through natural manifestations played a great role in creating Godliness among people of the earlier generations. Their judgement will also be according to their conscience. The incidents of the times of Noah and Nimrod explains the direct intervention of God. Up to the times of Mosaic covenants people lived according to their conscience worshipping God and sacrificing. Without the Mosaic law there is a universal law that is revealed to every human being through nature (Romans 1:18-22). He who walks in the way of the Lord shall be saved. Lot was saved. Because he was said to be righteous. Peter says it. Moreover, Abraham knew that Lot was righteous even if he was living in a country of blemishes; we see that in his plea for Lot before God. The life of Lot was saved, but not the salvation of his spirit. During the time of Noah, God destroyed the earth because of the wickedness of man (Genesis 6). Then enters a covenant for the whole earth and the children of Noah. [Covenant with Noah Genesis 9]. To walk in the way of God is the rule for man to follow. To shed the blood of another human being is sin because man is made in the image of God. That means respect and love for the other human beings is the basic behavioral rule of life. Also, not to eat blood which represents life when you eat animal flesh. It is seen that so far, humankind was thriving on vegetable, plants, fruits and tubers. It is only after the flood that, man was allowed to eat living animals. Up to Moses the law was not specific about sin and divine holiness. So far, God was dealing with whole world, selecting his righteous people, and giving them guidance. So, the general law for all the world from Adam, Noah, Abraham up to Moses was the same. [The covenant with Adam Genesis: 1: 28- 29 and 2: 15- 17]. First, through the Adamic covenant God revealed His plan for all humankind. God is to be worshipped and obeyed for the sake of His glory and greatness and for their own wellness or fearless living. The fear factor was there because of God's punishments then and there administered through nature. The concept of eternity or salvation was not a concern of the original inhabitants even though God's intention of salvation through the seed of the woman was revealed. "There always has been a way for honest people to be right with their Creator—if they seek after him and choose to please him (Acts 17:27ff). God so loved the entire world and gave his Son as a potential redeeming sacrifice for all who avail themselves of his gift (John 3:16). He is the loving benefactor to everyone who submits to his will in faithful obedience (1 Timothy 2:4; Hebrews 5:8-9; cf. 2 Peter 3:9)". -quote. In addition, the prophets clearly revealed Jehovah's redemptive concern for the Gentiles, who were to be grafted into the New Testament church on an equal basis with the Jews.

Eternity as Salvation

With Noah, God covenants for him and his descendants. Covenants are seen personal in nature. It is so with Abraham and his descendants. 'And in thy seed shall all the nations of earth be blessed; because thy hast obeyed my voice (Genesis 22:17-18)'. Here we see a promise for a blessed future for his generations. The entire humankind was one in nature prior to the call of Abraham

> *Revelations 22:13-I am Alpha and Omega, the beginning and the end, the first and the last.*
>
> *These terms speak of the Lords eternal existence, nature, and being. And by eternal, God means from all eternity past to all eternity future. Any one who isn't that kind of eternal isn't the Lord God, creator of heaven and earth.*
> *— David Sanford*

and even after, while his generations were blessed particularly. He was called the first Hebrew as seen in Bible (Genesis 14:13). The Hebrews were not set apart as a separate people until the giving of the law through Moses (Exodus 19:5-6; cf. Ephesians 2:14). It would be unrealistic if we do not accept that God's love for the Gentiles was a part of the ancient world. Further, with David(1 Chronicle17), we notice the promise of an eternal Kingdom- His covenant was 'But I will settle him in mine house and in my kingdom forever; and his throne shall be established *for evermore* (1 Chronicle 17:14)'. The 'eternity' factor here was veiled from discernment even for the Israelites. Even though we cannot see the concept of salvation and eternal life clearly revealed in the OT books it is inscribed in the hearts of godly people of the OT period (Ecclesiastes 3:11) and vaguely to God's chosen ones (e.g., Daniel 12:3-4 and many Psalms). Enoch being taken to heaven is an example for those people to have an idea of the heavenly realms. When Joseph gave directions to his brothers to take his bones from Egypt, he had a vision of eternity. Salvation in its present meaning was not a theme for OT books because that mystery was hidden and kept for the perfection of time for it to be revealed. Man being made in the image of God; eternity is also in his heart [Ecclesiastes 3:11]. The patriarchs were said to have lived with hope of eternity even though we do not see it to be offered in the covenants specifically. Their faith is honored by God. It is also specified in the book of Hebrew that they are waiting for perfection of salvation along with us [Hebrew 11:9-10, 39-40].

Hebrew for salvation is *yesua* (ה‎ע‎וש‎י) meaning deliverance, aid, victory, prosperity, saving, health, welfare etc. mostly seen in OT and *tesua* (ה‎ע‎ו‎ש‎ת‎) meaning rescue, deliverance. In most cases it is to represent material or physical safety and deliverance. This word is very wide in nature. The word *yasha* is a simple verb meaning to be open, wide, or free also dictionary meaning to deliver. *Haya* (ה‎י‎ה‎) and *yasa* (ה‎ש‎י) is the word mostly used in OT to mean save.

Greek word for salvation -σωτηρία - *sotería* meaning rescue and safety, salvation (physical or moral) and *soter* meaning deliverer.

Salvation in OT

Salvation in OT was related to security, safety and protection of person and possessions as we have already seen. Covenants also provides for prosperity. The contexts in Old Testament, where the word save or redeem were used, mostly point to deliverance from enemies and natural calamities and protection of their body and materials. Physical and material wellness were the main concerns during those days. Promises were for mainly the primary needs safety and security. As regards the common people God was a protector of them and their belongings. The words for salvation used in Hebrew and Greek are extensive to contain all spiritual and material meanings. In the course of time, we see the meaning of salvation converging to spiritual levels, on the advent of the Holy Spirit. And also, the concept of heaven and hades are more clearly portrayed in the NT even though there are vague pointers in Psalms and other poetic and prophetic books. When Job says, 'Though he slays me, yet will I trust in him; but I will maintain mine own ways before him' (Job 13:15), 'For I know that my redeemer lives, and that he shall stand at the latter day upon the earth. (Job 19:25-27). Job expresses his hope of encountering God at some time in the future. In verse 26 some translation uses the phrase 'yet in my flesh' whereas ASV and BBE (Bible in basic English) it is written as 'without my flesh'. I like the latter translation, which is seen in many versions, because the resurrected body is not in flesh, it is spirit. Job declares his hope of seeing God in His eternal tabernacle. As time passed by, we see the meaning of salvation converging to spiritual levels.

When Adam was created, he was promised eternal life in person to reign over everything on the earth. He was blessed for that [Genesis: 1: 28]. The condition was that he will die if he disobeys the law. His death was separation from God. His glorified personality transformed to just material and physical personality which is perishable. God wants to regain his creation to its original glory and magnificence. It is the love and mercy of God towards man. The process God employed since the eviction of Adam and Eve from Paradise to restore it to man is called salvation. It is evident from Eden that there itself God revealed his intention by dressing them with the skin of an animal, a sacrifice shedding blood, which is the symbol of life [Genesis: 3:21]. This action of God points towards forgiveness and salvation through sacrifice. But still, the sinned flesh shall return to dust.

In Old Testament, we cannot see repentance of Sin and Salvation. There is recompense for sin and forgiveness, as per the covenant with Israel through Moses. To appease God sacrifice was done even by the second generation. In Abrahamic covenant the sign of covenant is circumcision (Genesis 1:17); The condition is to do righteousness and justice. Genesis 18:19 '...shall keep the way of the lord, to do justice and judgment ...'. Because the people of Sodom did not walk in the way of Lord, the Lord destroyed it. The punishment for disobedience was given in the person and material of the people when it came to the level for the intervention of God.

Mosaic covenant was for a nation God selected for himself through Abraham, to be a model for the whole world. The previous laws and covenants were for individuals to follow; But in Mosaic laws it is not a personal covenant, but it is communal [Exodus: 32:10]. God affirms his promise to Abraham on their way to Canaan in the wilderness when they were in the Sinai dessert. In the Theophany of Sinai, God reveals himself to Moses and the multitude of Israelites [Exodus 19:4-25]. God reveals his greatness, strength and power and his divine holiness. Ten commandments and the rules and regulations for Israel were given which was read out to the people and they assured that they will obey God's words [Exodus 24]. But coming to chapter 32, the people are seen worshiping idols. The Levites begin to punish the people and the punishment for sin was given to their life and possessions. We do not see chances for repentance and forgiveness. The Levites were honored for their action [Numbers 3:5-13]. God wanted to destroy the whole Israel, but Moses pleads for them. And God changes his decision. Also, the Levites gets exemption from their curses [Genesis 34: 25, 49:5-7]. The Grace of God is also manifested here. In the process of covenants from Adam to Moses the divine grace is seen overflowing ever since.

Since the breach or violation of the law by Adam, the tendency of man was transgression. In between, some people in each generation are getting the favor of God. When the whole earth was filled in wickedness, Noah got favor of God, and was redeemed with his family. Here also, the Grace of God is at work. Again, the patriarchs received the grace of God. Israel as nation enjoyed it many times. They escaped destruction as Moses received the grace of God. By the grace of God, Aaron is selected for priesthood. God promised priesthood to his descendants. During the OT periods, before Moses, God communicated to people who walked in the ways of God to reveal his will. David too is enjoying the grace all through his life. Even though the grace of God originally was bestowed on the seed of Abraham, it is descending to David as per Davidic covenant, to be called the generation of David. Finally, Mary was addressed 'Hail thou that are highly favored' [Luke 1:28] for, Jesus is to be called the son of David. God promised an eternal kingdom to David which is fulfilled in Jesus. (Davidic covenant [2 Samuel 7, 1 Chronicles: 17:11- 14, 2 Chronicles 6:16]. The promise to Abraham is also seen fulfilled in Jesus.].

God created man in his own image; But we understand that God is spirit, and no physical image can be attributed to God. So, man is created in the spiritual image of God and hence the traits of man may involve the attributes of God. Hence, it is inevitable that the ways of God are innate or intrinsic in man. As the curse on earth came consequent to the violation of God's word by Adam, the thorn, and thistles also entered the mind and heart of man. It is evident in the vignette of Cain and Abel. So, in the former generations God's expectations about man might be to live by the words of God according to their conscience which is the built-in divine trait in human beings. The rule to walk in righteousness in the ways of God was universal. Abraham received favor from God because he walked faithful in the ways of God as per his conscience. Probably, Abraham, as for all his generations got the chance of knowing the great God of Noah. Why others failed to be elected by God? All the generations had the same chance of knowing God. Abraham too was from a family of idolators. But when God revealed himself to Abraham, because of his faithfulness in life and his righteous activities, he scrupulously obeyed the word of God in his life. This made him eligible to entering a covenant with God. The covenant was of the nature of a suzerain covenant. God in the dominating authority dictating the terms. From Edenic covenant and covenant with Noah, the same was the nature of covenant but all for the benefit and wellbeing of the party with whom God entered a covenant. The position was like that of a protectorate.

The patriarchs were said to have lived with hope of eternity even though we do not see it to be offered in the covenants specifically. Their faith is honored by God. It was only the grace of God that revealed an eternity to them. It is also specified in NT book of Hebrew that they are waiting for perfection of salvation nevertheless only along with us. 'By faith he sojourned in the land of promise, as in a strange country, dwelling in tabernacles with Isaac and Jacob, the heirs with him of the same promise: For he looked for a city which has foundations, whose builder and maker is God. [Hebrew: 11: 9- 10], 'And these all, having obtained a good report through faith, received not the promise: God having provided some better thing for us that they without us should not be made perfect [Hebrew 11:39- 40].

When sin has intruded into the life of Adam, his progenies who were born from the sinned soul and body also got stained with sin from their birth. But the original spirit that was breathed into the body is still there. And that spirit functions in every human at any time. Those who ignore the spirit walk in sinful ways allowing his spirit to be controlled by Satan. This we observe in the life of Cain and Abel. The sacrifice that covered the sin of Adam and Eve, Abel selected to please God. He walked in righteous ways pleasing to God. Cain also was inherently having the same spirit in him, but he chose to ignore it and walk in his own ways of sin. The heredity of Adam is counted through Seth. In that genealogy, as the sixth generation, Enoch was born. Enoch walked with God. We see that through generations the spirit of God continues to work. An eternal covenant is to be established through the seed of Abraham which points to a Messiah [Genesis: 12: 1- 3, 22: 18].

The OT deals with the history of two sets of people, i) who were guided by their conscience and ii) who were controlled by the Law. The period with law and without law comprising two millennia each. Up to Abraham from Adam is said to be about one thousand five hundred years and from Abraham to The Law, it is about five hundred. Till the end of prophesies, it is about one thousand six hundred years and from then up to Jesus is four hundred years. We call these four hundred years "The Silent period". Even despite it being called the silent period, during this period there transpired great developments in various intellectual, philosophical, and gnostic studies. Jews had been trained by law to the understanding and conviction of sin and its consequences. Heathens developed intellectually, literally and philosophically to the utmost and reached its full height. The influence of foreign rulers such as Persian and Greek had made great influence in world culture, civilization and thinking of gentile and religious people. The Roman political situation was also disturbed, and Judea was seeking a redeemer for Israel. All these situations constituted the opportune time for the spread of the Gospel due to the permeation of Greek language in the European and Asian countries. Here again it is two millennia after the law up to Jesus. Why is it called the Fullness of Time (Galatians: 4:4)? It is even more the pre-determined time of God as the right time to establish His decisions about humankind. No doubt His wisdom is great and surpasses all human knowledge and conception. God's timeline is different from human timeline. He is eternal and we are temporal.

Salvation in NT

Only through the NT we can understand the mystery of the covenant with Abraham. The persons with whom the covenant was made might not have foreseen the ultimate resolve of God. They in faith just lead a life righteous and lawful before God. Their blessed life on earth is attributed to their trust in God. The covenant with Abraham is passed over through God's selected people in generations as we see in Matthew chapter one to culminate in Mary, wife of Joseph, who is of the tribe, Judah. Righteousness of God also is seen in the genealogy of Jesus in the inclusion of four non-Israelite women in the list. -- Tamar, Rahab, Ruth and Bathsheba who, of the OT period, in accordance with their conscience and faith got included in the genealogy of Jesus. It was the scarlet thread of salvation that saved Rahab and her family when Jericho was destroyed (Joshua2:21ff). The historical period from Jesus Christ, is called Grace period. The curse of the law is faded off. A new covenant written in blood in human hearts is established. To implement the law a steward is appointed – the Holy Spirit. The offer to become the children of God is open to all human beings. No restrictions based on cast or creed or color or religion is imposed.

> *Faith in the Lord Jesus Christ is the foundation upon which sincere and meaningful repentance must be built. If we truly seek to put away sin, we must first look to Him who is the Author of our salvation.*
>
> *– Ezra Taft Benson*

Only the acceptance of the offer by believing in *heart* that the blood of Jesus has washed away all my sins and he saved me from the bondage of Satan, is required.

In prophetic books the advent of a redeemer, a *Messiah,* is predicted. But Israel could not comprehend the concept fully. They evaluated the prophecy in the context of their bondage to the Roman empire. The gospel of the Kingdom of God and of transformation came through John the Baptist. The meaning of redemption or salvation in its spiritual perspective becomes clear through the New Testament. As we consider the Old Testament the shadow of what is to come, and that which is prophesied having happened, and being revealed through New Testament books, we are fortunate to understand the meaning of redemption, justification, and salvation. That which was considered of materialistic in nature gave way to spirituality. The scarlet thread that was in shadow in the OT became distinct in the New Testament when Jesus said, 'this cup is the new covenant in my blood'. The law that was made for a nation became obsolete and a new law written in the heart of human beings with the blood of the sacrificial lamb gained over it. Hereafter we see the scarlet thread prominently displayed in the robe of righteousness, and garments of salvation with which the church, the bride of Jesus Christ, is to be adorned (Psalms 45:13-15).

"There always has been a way for honest people to be right with their Creator—if they seek after him and choose to please him (Acts 17:27ff). God so loved the entire world and gave his Son as a potential redeeming sacrifice for all who avail themselves of his gift (John 3:16). He is the loving benefactor to everyone who submits to his will in faithful obedience (1 Timothy 2:4; Hebrews 5:8-9; cf. 2 Peter 3:9)". In addition, the prophets clearly revealed Jehovah's redemptive concern for the Gentiles, who were to be grafted into the New Testament church on an equal basis with the Jews.

What do we as Christians understand as Salvation? The fundamental doctrine of salvation is considered as what is contained in Romans

10:9; confession with mouth and believing in heart. It is obtained by grace; it is the gift of God and not by the works of man. (Ephesians 2:5,8). Jesus told the Sadducees 'You are in error because you do not know the Scripture or the power of God' (Matthew 22:29). This shall not become true for us. We are not expected to be ignorant of the Scripture and the *scarlet thread of redemption*. The theological meaning given for salvation is deliverance from sin and its consequences believed to be brought about by faith in Christ. According to Augustin of Hippo sin is "a word, deed or desire in opposition to the eternal Law of God". Because of the ancestral sin humankind is born enslaved to sin. The consequence of sin is death as per Edenic covenant and it is reiterated by Apostle Paul (Romans 6:23). Here death is the separation of man from God. The total depravity of humankind is resolved by the grace of God through Jesus Christ, and it is called redemption. A covenant is cut between God and man through the precious blood of Jesus Christ. All the sacrifices we have seen in OT was image of this human sacrifice as a lamb without any blemishes. He is blameless and holy because the Father had set him apart as his own for the purpose of becoming recompence for the sin of humankind (John 10:36). The Law of God requires that the sacrificial lamb shall be without blemishes. Salvation is responding positively to the grace of God revealed through the sacrifice of Jesus Christ His only begotten son. It is getting reconciled or to be at par with the *holiness* of God through faith in Jesus Christ and in his sacrifice and resurrection. This is the plan of God for man to return to the lost paradise.

How can we know that we are in the true path of salvation? Only if we love God and obey His words. First, 'Love the Lord thy God with all thy heart, and with all thy soul and with all thy mind and with all thy strength'

> *To gain strength in our struggles, we must have a positive perspective of the principles in the plan of salvation. We must realize that we have a personal Savior whom we can trust and turn to in our times of need.*
>
> *– L. Lionel Kendrick*

and the second is, 'thy shall love thy neighbor as thyself' (Mark 12:30-31). 'If a man loves me, he will keep my words, and my Father will love him, and we will come unto him and make our abode with him' (John 14:23). If we can enjoy this glorious experience, then we are in the right path. Our faith shall be wholehearted. We must surrender all our body, soul, and spirit to Jesus our savior. We must cleanse ourselves from all blemishes by repenting and washing in the blood of Jesus to get justified and reconciled to God.

Because the core and central theme of Bible is deliverance from the bondage of sin or the power of Satan, which ultimately leads to the "perfection of salvation" it would be better to study the subject redemption and salvation in detail. There are four steps to reach the perfection of salvation as described by Paul in Romans 8:30.

1)Predestination 2) Calling 3) Justification and 4) Glorification. The first two steps God had already done. When Jesus was born the message by the angel about the Savior was". behold, I bring you good tidings of great joy, which shall be to all people" (Luke 2:10-11). Now it is our part to accept Justification by faith and repentance. Now we become dead to sin and alive to God in Jesus Christ (Romans 6:11). How shall we, that are dead to sin, live any longer therein? (6:2) 'I have been crucified with Christ and I no longer live, but Christ lives in me' (Galatians 2:20). This shall be the life of a Christian who is redeemed to get qualified for glorification. Nothing short of it will suffice.

Illustrations of Salvation in OT and NT

Again, we shall go to some illustrations from OT and NT. First let me draw your attention to the episode of the deliverance of Israelites from Egypt. The, then Pharaoh was cruel to the Israelites and their cry reached God. Moses was assigned with duty of drawing them out of Egypt and establish them in another land which was already promised to them through Abraham. God instructed the Israelites to observe Passover to escape from the striking of the first born of all men and beast of the Egyptians. All of us are familiar with the incidents and accept it as an example of deliverance from sin through the blood of Jesus. It is confirmed by Paul when he states 'Christ our Passover lamb has been crucified for us' (1 Corinthians 5:7). Our faith in Jesus Christ brings us salvation. The redemption from the slavery is the result of a onetime act of observing Passover. But they, the Israelites are not allowed to continue there in Egypt thinking that Pharaoh is given due punishment by God and so he will not be cruel to them anymore; also, they can get employment with more facilities and incentives. Moreover, Moses could be made their leader to deal with Pharaoh when labor problems arise in future. The redeemed are to *leave all the present situations* for they are redeemed to be re-established in another land with an identity for themselves. Until this purpose of God for them is completed they have nowhere to linger or dally. Redemption is only the first step in the process. Those who are redeemed must make themselves ready to leave behind every surroundings in which they were slaves so that the atmosphere shall not influence them anymore. They must obey the new leader whom they got convinced to be capable of leading them to the promised land. Promised land is not a temporary abode but for all their coming generations too. So, the redeemed are to be re-established. They are redeemed from slavery to become a separate people for God. I will ordain a place for *my people Israel*, and will plant them, and they shall dwell in their place, and shall be moved no more; neither shall the children of wickedness waste them anymore, as at the beginning (1 Chronicle 17:9). Likewise, those who are redeemed by the blood of Jesus Christ shall crucify the old man in their flesh with all its lusts and desires. The journey, to possess that land, is a temporary affair for they will reach the destination in a short while. It was only 11 days journey to Kadesh Barnea (Deutronomy 1:2). But they had to wander in the desert forty years because of their unfaithfulness. During that journey they have to understand who God is and how He will provide and protect them. It is to teach them how they are special to God and how God loves them. This period of journey is the time required to be qualified for the new land by making themselves clean from the desires of flesh. 'Sanctify yourselves; For the Lord will do wonders among you' (Joshua 3:5). To enter the promised land, where the Lord has given them rest, they have to sanctify themselves. In the desert God wanted to teach them how they should behave with their brethren and others and how they should respond to God's instructions. But they lusted, committed fornication, they tempted God and murmured against God. That led them to their destruction and all of them perished in the desert. This is written for our admonition and as examples for us (1 Corinthians 10:1-11). The fact we have to think of is, that all of them were redeemed through the blood of the Passover lamb. What I mean to say of redemption, is a once for all activity of drawing us from the pit of sin. Then we have to live a life of spiritual faith for the perfection of salvation, which we will gain in glorification with Jesus Christ. We have to go a long way to be assured of salvation. The desert life gives us chance to learn the word of God and understand the Almighty God and experience him. We have to cross the Jordan, a true transformation, the true baptism that Jesus had gone through, which he asked his disciples whether they could experience that baptism or could they drink the cup He drinks. Then cross the Jordan and wash away all the reproaches of Egypt, experience the Gilgal and get reconciled with God. Then only we can lead a holy Christian life. In that life you have to face Jericho, fight the enemies to possess our inheritance. For us the enemies are not of this world; 'we wrestle not against flesh and blood, but against principalities, against powers, against the rulers of the darkness of this world, against spiritual wickedness in high places' (Ephesians 6:12). They have to toil in the grounds for their livelihood. It was not the case in the wilderness; they got everything they asked for in the desert, they were living in all comforts, but God sent leanness into their soul (Psalms 106:15). Christian life is not a life in the desert but a life in Canaan, where we get peace and rejoicing in the midst of persecutions or hardships. We experience fellowship of Christ's sufferings, for being made conformable unto his death to become partakers of his resurrection (Philippians 3:10). Paul had the desert life of three years to learn the scriptures and he became conformed to Jesus Christ in his life through various sufferings. 'Not as though I had already attained, either were already perfect but I follow after, if that I may apprehend that for which also, I am apprehended of Christ Jesus' (Philippians 3:12). His true Christian life lead him at last to say 'I had fought a good fight, I have finished my course, I have kept the faith: (2 Timothy 4:7). Even this experience is the assurance of salvation only. Still, we cannot say we are saved but only that we are redeemed from sin, which does not mean we have passed the test of salvation. 'I am crucified with Christ: nevertheless, I live; yet not I, but Christ lives in me; and the life which I now live in the flesh I live by the faith of the Son of God, who loved me, and gave himself for me' (Galatians 2:20). This is the testimony that a redeemed Christian is expected to have in his life. Jesus said, 'If a man loves me, he will keep my words: and my father will love him, and we will come unto him, and make our abode with him' (John 14:23) - The Father and Son abiding in the redeemed person if he loves Jesus and His words. True Christian life is Canaan experience. All reproaches of Egypt are washed away at Gilgal the gateway of Canaan. Even in Canaan there is chances of failure as the Israel has failed. In Canaan Israel has to face tests and tribulations and show perseverance to possess their inheritance. They were commanded that they shall destroy all the gentiles there; but they failed to obey God's command. Our inheritance, the kingdom of God, we have to possess by fighting our enemy, Satan. The completion of salvation is in the kingdom.

Three Types of People

Natural Man

Another illustration is seen in the epistles of Paul, about three different types of men whom we can relate to the life in Egypt, travel in desert up to Jordan and Canaan life. First is the *natural man*, who cannot understand spiritual things. 'But the natural man receives not the things of the spirit of God: for they are foolishness unto him: neither can he know them, because they are spiritually discerned' (1 Corinthians 2:14). The heathen and even the heirs of Abraham in Egypt belonged to this group of natural man.

Man of Flesh

When the children of Abraham were redeemed through the Passover process their status changed. But all through their life in the desert they were *men of flesh*. We do not see any spiritual change in them even though they know God as their protector. They continued to rebel against Moses and God. Throughout the journey God wanted them to be holy. God manifests through miracles and provide for all their needs so that the redeemed shall qualify to enter Canaan. They are still controlled by

> *The greatest enemy to human souls is the self-righteous spirit which makes men look to themselves for salvation.*
>
> *– Charles Spurgeon*

the desires of their flesh. They fight and quarrel even though they were redeemed. This nature we see among the redeemed New Testament people too. This is the second category of people who are seen among redeemed Christians also not only now but even among first century churches too - Men of flesh. James admonishes the Jewish Christians (James 4:1-3). Paul writes to the Corinthian Christians that he cannot address them as spiritual people. They are still worldly, he says. There is jealousy and quarrelling among them and they are like mere humans – they are of flesh. This letter he writes to the church of God in Corinth. (1 Corinthians 3:1-3). It is clear that this was the nature of Israelites in the wilderness that caused them to be perished in the wilderness. So, claiming to be redeemed from sin only is not sufficient to be a Christian, it is growing in Christ that brings salvation. We have to grow in the word of God daily. We should be able to assimilate solid food rather than still drinking milk as babies. We have to be perfect in divine knowledge and wisdom to perfect our salvation.

Man of Spirit

The third group is the *Man of Spirit* who discern spiritual things. The law of the spirit comes through Jesus Christ. Flesh shall not weaken the power of spirit. The man of spirit acquires a complete translation from carnal thoughts to thoughts of the Spirit. (Romans 8:1-10). He lives according to the spirit and not according to flesh. This is the nature of life expected in Canaan. Canaan signifies a life of faith having the assurance of eternity. There too we have to face and wrestle against temptations but shall not fail. 'If we deliberately keep sinning after we have received the knowledge of truth, no sacrifice for sins is left' (Hebrews 10:26). We can hence arrive at a conclusion that Salvation is not redemption, but it is a package leading to the eternal life through spiritual perfection. Also, I request my dear readers not to

> *There is never time in the future in which we will work out our salvation. The challenge is in the moment; the time is always now.*
>
> *— James Baldwin*

compare your life with life in the desert. We are not called to stay in a comfort zone enjoying this mortal life. We are redeemed to do the will of our father and finish his work to his satisfaction and not to pray God always to work for our satisfaction. When we submit ourselves to His will, He will accomplish His promise of satisfying all our needs in this world and will re-establish us in the Kingdom of God which is *"paradise regained"*.

Conclusion

Most people discern salvation as a once for all process in Christian life. A certain group of people consider it a developing or a continuous process in Christian life. Another group thinks it as a chain of pearls which together accounts for achieving salvation. Still further a small group accepts it as a thread having a beginning and an end. It is true that the Bible refers to salvation differently according to contexts. This scarlet thread is a thread of blood. Blood is mentioned hundreds of times in the Bible, throughout both the Old and New Testaments. A man's life is in the blood; the price for sin is blood; atonement for sin comes only through the blood of the Messiah; and the blood reaches from the depths of sin to the courts of heaven

The spiritual growth expected of a redeemed believer towards salvation can be explained simply by the following diagrammatic representation: -

Egypt → Redemption and desert →Canaan →Rest (eternity)

Natural man→ Man of flesh→ Spiritual man or man of calling→Perfection of Salvation on resurrection.

Further we see redemption in its literal meaning in the case of Bar - Abbas who was *saved* from his death punishment for his crime whereas the thief on the cross got *eternal salvation* accepting earthly punishment of death. Here, we see the scarlet thread connecting salvation as per both the covenants. Bar-Abbas in my view represents all the people redeemed from Egypt and the so called redeemed of the NT period. The meaning of the name is "son of the father" which is generic in nature and not specific. We do not have any future details of that man whether he lived as a Christian or a Jew. He represents a redeemed person like me or you. It is for a Christian believer to ponder whether his own story ends as that of Bar- Abbas or continues to eternity. Hereafter the new covenant starts from the covenant in blood of Jesus Christ. It is well explained and established in the epistles, more specifically in the book of Hebrews.

The book of Hebrews emphasizes the establishment of the new covenant for salvation and its perfection in the place of the old Mosaic Law which was imperfect and obsolete. About the righteous people of the OT period the author states '.... these were all commended for their faith, yet none of them received what have been promised, since God had planned something better for us so that only *together **with us would they be made perfect'*** (Hebrews 11:39-40). Salvation is not perfected in this world, but we can have the assurance of salvation in this world itself. All the saints are still waiting for the perfection of salvation, and we will also join them on resurrection. The scarlet thread of salvation, we see is a progressive process running from Aden throughout the history of humankind till it ends up with the regaining of the lost paradise.

We see four non-Israelite women also in this thread, Tamar, Rahab, Ruth, and Bathsheba who, of the OT period, in accordance with their conscience and faith included in the genealogy of Jesus. It was the scarlet thread of salvation that saved Rahab and her family when Jericho was destroyed (Joshua 2:21ff). In many of the Psalms we can see the hope of an eternal life with God. One of the verses that I Love to repeat in my mind is Psalms 42:1. The hope for an eternal life with God is manifested here.

Many Christian believers consider faith only as a grip to hold in times of necessities. Some people hold on to this 'religion' rather "The Way," only because they are born in that religion. Some people consider their ministry as a

> *What I would say is Jesus came to save lost sinners like you and me, and if Jesus Christ has a burning desire to seek and save the lost, then you should, too, if Christ is living within you. If you don't have a concern for the lost, then I am concerned about your salvation because the Holy Spirit wants the lost to come to Christ.*
>
> *– Kirk Cameron*

vocation only. And others in all other ways according to their selfish motives except in spiritual ways. Spirituality comes as a last resort when everything else has failed. It is just a trial then. True faith in heart only can bring the experience of salvation. 'By no means! We are those who have died to sin; how can we live in it any longer? (Romans 6:2). The baptism that Jesus accomplished in cross, and the resurrection is the experience of baptism a person with the assurance of salvation is having (Luke 12:50). In the end Jesus Christ will hand over the kingdom to the Father along with all the redeemed and saved saints. 'Then comes the end, when he delivers the kingdom to God the Father after destroying every rule and every authority and power. For he must reign until he has put all his enemies under his feet' (1 Corinthians 15:24). Jesus said to disciples if they leave everything of this world on accord of Jesus, they will be provided with everything they have left, in hundred folds in this world itself and in the eternal world. It is the promise of Jesus, and he is able to do that. But why we could not experience or enjoy it, because our faith is often a farce. Jesus asked Peter ' do you love me more than these? If we can answer from our heart an emphatic "Yes Lord, I love you" then we are blessed.

2

Glorious Grace

We may say we rejoice in the salvation gifted to us by the great sacrifice of Jesus Christ on the cross. Have we gone into the nucleus or crux of the word we call – 'Salvation'? We talk over the technicalities of the word and the mechanism of getting saved. Does it make any changes in our lives? Are we concerned with the spiritual aspects and its wonderful acts of transformation?

St. Paul in Ephesians 2:5 says, "… by grace you are saved…". So, salvation is the primary and ultimate result of the grace of God, and I may equate salvation to the grace of God which leads us through to stand blameless and pure before Him. In chapter 1 of the same book he says we are adopted as children through Jesus Christ for the purpose "to praise the glory of his grace". In this verse, I find the title of the article and the meaning of the word 'Salvation'. I have heard many people use the word 'grace' referring to material gains and spiritual blessings, and for any gifts they enjoy in life all alike. According to my conception of the word it is inclusive of all these things but above all it is the deal that God made to transfer our ownership for himself. By birth, because of the Adamic sin we are all born to this world of sin, and we became of the world. Originally, we belonged to the Almighty God, but Satan played the trick to covet Adam and Eve to use for his purpose of thwarting God's plan. In my opinion, we can see two things where

Adam failed. 1. In Genesis 1:28 we see that man was to subdue and exercise dominion over all what God created.2. Genesis 2:15 it says Adam was placed in the garden of Eden to tend it . Adam failed to protect the garden from intruders and failed to subdue the serpent over which also he was given dominion. Our Creator wanted to reinstate the fallen man in his original glory through a proper lawful deal. *From paradise to paradise lost and back to paradise regain.* When the transaction is completed by paying the price not in gold or silver but with a ransom most valuable, not any one in this world has ever given, the life of the only beloved and begotten son as a sacrifice, we are owned by the purchaser. Thence we are to be used for the purpose of our owner and we are not our own or of this world. By this deed of God all are given the chance to become his children with one condition to believe that I am purchased through the blood of Jesus Christ. *Although all human beings are the creation of God only those who believe in Jesus Christ and the salvation through his blood only have the right to become children of God and claim inheritance to the Kingdom of God.* When our ownership and parenthood has changed, we are to live according to the will of our father who adopted us. Our life is for the satisfaction of his will, not for our satisfaction. Our thoughts shall not be of concern for ourselves but to be for the satisfaction of our master and owner. God who works everything for good to his children wants us to be fully aware and confident of this truth. (Romans 8:28). He has got some special purpose for all his children. To accomplish that he may lead us through different paths which he knows best. It may sometimes seem difficult for us to move on, but he will enable us to overcome it as his eyes are always on us and his ways are perfect. The comprehension of the purpose of God for us and our submission to his will leads us to rejoice in God's grace working in us. How great is his love for us! How amazing it is! Along with David I too may confess that 'He lifted me out of the slimy pit, out of the mud and mire; he set my feet on a rock and gave me a place to stand'. That rock is Jesus Christ. As John Newton sang, it is his amazing grace that saved a wretch like me…., or as Paul says I am the first of those sinners. Anne Lamott an American author wrote, "I do not at all understand the mystery of grace- only that it meets us where we are but does not leave us where it found us."

Grace is the ability to face any situation God allows us to go through with rejoicing and praising. 'And, they departed from the presence of the council, rejoicing that they were counted worthy to suffer shame for his name'. (Acts 5:41)-This is 'grace' – to persevere and rejoice in sufferings and shame for the sake of Jesus Christ.

In the present Christian arena, we use the word 'grace' as synonym for all worldly and material gains to exhibit us as spiritual persons and to claim that we are blessed by God. We account God's mercy, kindness, and all goodness we enjoy as the grace of God. May be, all of it we receive because of God's grace on us. By considering our worldly and material wellbeing as the grace of God there is a tendency to underestimate the cost that Jesus paid for our redemption. So, we are devaluing the true grace of God. Is not this a pretense, sheer humbug? Are we not trying to project us sanctimoniously before people around us? Beware, we know the fate of the fig tree cursed by Jesus. All those material gains and worldly achievements Paul rejected as dung when he experienced the grace.

God adopted us as his children even before the foundation of the world. Of course, there is great difference between natural children and adopted ones. Suppose a doctor or nurse brings a child born in the hospital and says to its parents, "Sir, here is your baby", the parent has no right to say, "I don't like this baby, get me some other good-looking healthy child". No. He must accept the baby. But in the case of adoption, the person who adopts has the right to choose a child of his choice. The great God who adopted us is the alpha and omega, the beginning, and the end, and He sees and knows everything of a man, as of now, because he is eternal. He is not limited to the earthly dimensions. He created the sun, moon, and stars for measuring day and time for man. God is beyond time dimensions, and our timings are not of any effect in God's realm. He knows who we are and who we should be. He assigned the *SWOT* things for us. Knowing our strength, weaknesses, opportunities, and threats, which are the attributes he has allotted to us. He knew our substance even before we were born in the womb of our mother." My substance was not hid from thee, when I was made in secret, and curiously wrought in the lowest parts of the earth. Thine eyes did see my substance, yet being unperfect; and in thy book all my members were written, which in continuance were fashioned, when as yet there was none of them". (Psalms 139:15-16). It is the greatest wonder that God had done to release us from the bondage of the prince of darkness – The gift of grace. The adoption through the sacrifice of his only begotten son is 'Grace', and that is in other words 'Salvation'. Also, he made us "sit together in heavenly places in Christ Jesus" (Ephesians : 2: 5-9, Colossians: 1: 12-13). And made us partakers of the inheritance of saints in light. For that he has translated us into the kingdom of his dear son. He foreknew us and did predestinate us to conform to the image of His son (Romans 8:29). This we understand to be the glorious grace.

Grace of Election

Grace of election is defined by various theologians differently. *The belief that God chooses for eternal salvation those whom, he foresees will exercise their free will to respond to God's divine grace that precedes human decisions with faith in Jesus Christ* is referred as Prevenient or preceding Grace. This preceding grace enables one to accept the grace of salvation, but it does not ensure salvation. This grace encourages one through various divine procedures to exercise his free will to accept or reject the salvific offer given through Jesus Christ.

Another doctrine about grace is Irresistible Grace that causes the chosen one to co-operate, believe, repent and to come freely and willingly to Jesus Christ. This saving grace God effectively and purposefully applies to his elect ones overcoming all impediments that may resist his salvation and bring him to the gospel of salvation.

'Moreover, whom he did predestinate, them he called; and whom he called, them he also justified; and whom he justified, them he also glorified' (Romans 8:30). They are the called according to his purpose. If he has purposed, he is able to fulfill it regardless of the choice of the elect. Both the above doctrines we see current in the Christendom. God is almighty and he does according to his will – For he says to Moses 'I will have mercy on whom I have mercy, and I will have compassion on whom I have compassion' (Romans 9:5). God shows mercy not to all but to his chosen people. But we know that the grace is also open to all as per the word of God that '........ Yet to all who did receive him, to those who believed in his name, he gave the right to become children of God.........born of God (John 1:12-13). *The substitutionary atonement accomplished by Jesus is sufficient for all but is efficient for the elect only.*

"I am so glad that God chose me before the foundation of the world, because he never would have chosen me after I was born" - Spurgeon

*"God chose me for himself, but devil chose me for himself. My choice is the ice-breaker".D.L.*Moody.

The above statements by two great missionaries tell of some aspects of God's grace on His people - Election by God and choice by us. God gave this choice to Adam and Eve in the garden of Eden which still God gives us as He made us in His image and have honored our freedom of selection. The Bible nowhere instructs us to be concerned about our status of being elect or non-elect, rather we are advised to believe the gospel of his kingdom, believe in the salvation by grace through Jesus Christ. Those without Christ are blind to their need for salvation. Invitation is given to all, but the elects are a few. The elect will enjoy dinner with the bridegroom. The elects are entitled for gifts and blessings, the first gift being the Holy Spirit. When the called or invited choose to reject the invitation as the Jews neglected to turn up, God in his will is at liberty to invite from anywhere in the world to meet his purpose. It would be miserable if we lose our chance to be eligible for his grace of election. Our life on earth is just like a pebble in the fields or a bubble in the water. It fades like a shadow very easily. Many people are inclined to accept the gift of divine grace but delays the decision because the power of this world puts a siege on their minds restricting to take the decision. Love towards this world is the barrier. But once the bond is broken, we will be free, and the saving grace will take charge of our lives as we submit willingly and sincerely. We will be admitted to rejoicing and happiness in the presence of God Almighty and his provisions and protection. Our lives will not be futile . Our soul and body will be under the control of the Holy Ghost working through our human spirit. No more will our flesh direct our mind and spirit. How great an experience it will be when God the Father and Jesus Christ the Son living in us, that is to get identified with Jesus, the true Christian identity that gives meaning to the word Christianity!

Unmerited Grace

"Your human mind, with its philosophy of an equal return for favors done, can hardly comprehend the full meaning of this grace of God. But when you catch, by the inspiration of God, it's full meaning, you will leave the limits of human reasoning and revel in the spiritual riches of divine truth and privilege" Billy Graham

The Gospel declares that all people all over the world are forgiven their sins in Christ through his death on the cross and his glorious resurrection. According to the world it is beyond their reasoning. The thinking of the common man will be of a superhuman power to forgive the sins in response to sacrifice or recompense for the sin. So far that was the nature of God according to the OT covenants too. The covenants failed in its purpose of changing the heart of humans as it was related to the flesh with rituals and works. Those laws could not transform the spirit and mind and the works of sin in body. God himself coming to the world and becoming a recompense for the sins of all the world is a concept that is beyond the comprehension of the world. 'Christ hath redeemed us from the curse of the law, being made a curse for us…. For ye are all the children of God by faith in Christ Jesus' (Galatians 3:13,26). Paul says 'here is a trustworthy saying that deserves full acceptance: Christ Jesus came into the world to save sinners – of whom I am the worst' (1 Timothy1:15). Salvation through faith in Jesus Christ is the gift of grace. The offer is to all the world, and those who accept the offer and accomplish its terms and conditions can fully enjoy the benefits of grace. Faith is not just saying by word and speech, but it should be in truth and actions. Faith shall be revealed in actions. It is precisely stated in the book of James. We must prove our faith through our actions, behaviors, and manners. Faith without actions is a nullity. God's grace is promised to those who love God and those who are called according to God's purpose by everything being done for good in their lives. 'Whoever has my commands and keeps them is the one who loves me. The one who loves me will be loved by my father, and I too will love them and show myself to them' (John 14:21). These words of Jesus fulfill the condition stated in the words of Paul in Romans 8:28. God has done everything for humankind to reinstate them in the once lost paradise. He has offered his glorious grace to everyone in this world and those who accept and submit to His will can enjoy it. Jesus has come not to call the righteous but the sinners. We have become heirs for the kingdom of God not by the Mosaic Laws but by faith in Jesus through a covenant made with Abraham that 'through your offspring all nations on earth will be blessed, because you have obeyed me' (Genesis 22:18). Thus, our hierarchy is through Abraham who is known as the Father of Believers. Once we were addressed as Gentiles, but now we are children. Israel though they were the chosen people of God they were mostly referred as servants of God but those who are redeemed by the blood of Jesus are called children and heirs. 'So, you are no longer a slave, but God's child; and since you are his child, God has made you also an heir' (Galatians 4:7) and we also read 'The spirit you received does not make you slaves, so that you live in fear again; rather, the spirit you received brought about your adoption to sonship. And by him we cry, Abba, Father' (Romans 8:15). Praise the Lord for his wonderful works for us.

Yes, it is receiving blessings when we do not deserve it. Let us consider the examples of two persons in the Bible who received unmerited gifts from God.

First, the thief on the cross who got qualified to enter into the paradise at the last moments of his life just by repentance prompted by his awareness of the *Messiah* even though he was punished for the crimes committed . The grace he received is counted for his eternity and not for the life in this world. We can say he received the glorious grace of being with Jesus Christ in paradise. His prayer was "Jesus, lord, remember me when thou comest into thy kingdom". He was aware of the Messiah and the glory of being in the kingdom of God. He accepted his cross in peace and enjoyment of being with Jesus in paradise. He repented and he witnessed his faith to his immediate neighbor whereas his co-malefactor who was hanged asked for the rescue of his physical body. The thief who was saved experienced the grace of God to die peacefully and not to live or rescued from being punished. How can we count our earthly benefits as God's grace when we do not have a longing for his kingdom?

Second, we may think of Barabbas. He got a clean acquittal and was absolved from capital punishment without a petition or apology from his part. The choice before *Pontius Pilate* was either Barabbas or Jesus. We are not sure, or the Bible is silent as whether there was another choice other than Barabbas. His crime was proven with proper evidence. But there was no evidence against Jesus and Pilate confirmed Jesus' innocence thrice making it absolute that the scape- goat was perfect and without blemishes. Barabbas was released only because Jesus took his place . He was to go to Golgotha, may be, that day. He spent every passing hour thinking of that dreadful moment of his being hanged on the cross along with the other felons. Why or how he became eligible for freedom is beyond rationale. It is grace- divine grace only. Nothing is seen mentioned in Bible about his life after his release. He could have followed the ways of Jesus or continued his previous lifestyle. Why is the Bible silent about such an "important person". The meaning of the word Bar-abbas is 'son of the father'. Whether Barabbas happened to be the beneficiary of the *'Paschal pardon'* is a coincidence or divine plan, we must think seriously. The meaning of his name and the non-mention of his future life, requires each of us to replace our name in this historical incident. What should our future life be as we too are given freedom through Jesus Christ.? We claim to be the children of the almighty father. That is, we call ourselves Bar-abbases. We must complete the story of Barabbas by living a life pleasing to our father in His glorious grace.

We see the Roman centurion asking Jesus to heal his servant. He acknowledges his worthlessness before Jesus and says 'Lord, I do not deserve to have you to come under my roof. But just say the word ……….'. Jesus appreciates his faith. And the request of the centurion is granted. According to the Jewish people who knew the centurion he is an eligible candidate to receive his request from Jesus. To be eligible for grace of God first we must accept our inadequacy and then submit to the authority of God.

When the leper came to Jesus he said 'Lord. If you are willing…..'. Why did he say, "If you are willing"? He knows that according to the Jewish law he is not allowed to move in public. He is stamped as an unclean man. But he shows the courage to approach Jesus who has authority to cleanse him. He is aware of his undeserving status and is also aware of the Lord who is efficient and sufficient for his cause. To enjoy the grace of God we must be aware of our status before God and the nature of God who is kind and merciful.

Enabling Grace

By grace through faith in Jesus when we are saved, God enables us to lead a faithful Christian life. Where the Israelites failed to live according to the laws written on tablets, God gives us even the grace to observe the laws written on the hearts. The Israelites were more concerned about the literal observation of the law rather than trusting and obeying God in true spirit as God expected them. " .... But the word preached to them did not profit them, not being mixed with faith in them that heard it" (Hebrews 4:2). It is grace that saved us and enabled us to live faithfully before God. We have to submit ourselves to this enabling grace by accepting that we are no more our own, but we are bought with a price precious than the most valuable things in this world. We must live according to the will of him who purchased us. It is quite natural that anything purchased for value is for the exclusive use of the owner. "Know ye not that your body is the temple of the Holy Ghost, which ye have of God, and ye are not your own?" (1 Corinthians 6:19) He knows our nature as men of flesh. We on our own abilities cannot live according to the will of God. God wants us to be as holy as Himself to become heirs for the Heavenly Kingdom. He has given us the Holy Spirit to guide us through. He reminds us of what Jesus has taught, and gives us awareness of truth, righteousness, and judgement. God wants us to be Christ like. That is the reason why Jesus shed his blood for the salvation of humans – '...... to be conformed to the image of his son, that he might be the firstborn among many brethren'. To enable ourselves to live like Jesus we must identify the source of grace. Jesus said we are not of this world. We must separate ourselves from this world to be identified with Christ. It is our 'yes or no' to the world that enables us to separate us from this world. We need this grace every day to lead a Christian life which is a life of separation from world and consecration unto God. We have to cleave unto the Lord and enjoy the grace of God. Paul expresses his fear for Corinthians that 'your minds may somehow be led astray from your sincere and pure devotion to Christ' (2 Corinthians 11:3). God desires us to be always focused on Jesus Christ for, 'Those who looked at him are radiant; their faces are never covered with shame' (Psalm 34:5). When do we need the grace of God terribly? When our heart is broken, crushed, and bleeding as we face extreme situations of life. God's enabling grace is sufficient to console us and to enable us to remain steadfast in our faith. He has promised his eternal peace surpassing all the comforts we receive from any source in this world. Jesus Christ enabled Paul and he says, 'I thank Christ Jesus our Lord, who gave me strength, that he considered me trustworthy, appointing me to his service. Even though I was once a blasphemer and a persecutor and a violent man, I was shown mercy because I acted in ignorance and unbelief. The grace of our Lord was poured on me abundantly, along with the faith and love that are in Jesus Christ' (1 Timothy 1:12-14).

'For he chose us in him before the creation of the world to be holy and blameless in his sight. In love he predestined us for adoption to sonship through Jesus Christ, in accordance with his pleasure and will- to the praise of his glorious grace, which he has freely given us in the One he loves …… in accordance with the riches of God's grace that he lavished in us' (Ephesians 1:4-8).

But again, we have to be aware that God's grace is enabling grace and not ensuring grace. It is always available for us, but we receive it daily as we grow in spirit by putting aside every weight and throwing off the entangling sins and running our race towards the goal of eternal life steadfastly with patience and perseverance producing the fruit of spirit. It is our attitude to acknowledge the leadership of the Holy Spirit that works to grow in us all things such as sacrificial love, divine happiness, Godly peace, long suffering, kindness, favoring others, serene calmness, temperance, trust worthiness etc. Not only he has lavished his glorious grace on us, but he enables us to accomplish his purpose for us through divine blessings. God's enabling grace helps us to endure sufferings, share our God given gifts and goodness, forgive others and love others thereby manifesting God's love for us. He who loves God will not love the world. God's grace enables us to abstain from all the things of the world that are the lust of the flesh, and the lust of the eyes and the pride of life (1John 2:15-16).

Enduring grace

When we are elected to enjoy the grace of salvation, we are called to be partakers of the sufferings of Jesus Christ, only then can we claim to be with Jesus Christ in the resurrection. In addition to rejoicing in the glory of God we have to rejoice in our tribulations also. Our tribulations work in us leading us to a great experience of hope which coincides with the divine purpose for us. It enables us to persevere and to experience patience. That is the work of God's glorious grace in his elect people.

The concept of endurance means the ability to persevere or being steadfast or standing firm during the times of severe pain, afflictions, or torments. We all are subjected to periods of trials and difficulties. But as humans we get exhausted of our confidence or get desperate to the core or discouraged. Many people resort to giving up even their lives. Christians are not expected to go weary in such circumstances. Jesus set an example through his life in this world for how far we can withstand such situations. We see that Christ was so cast down as to be compelled to cry out in deep anguish: "My God, my God, why hast thou forgotten me?". He was wounded, oppressed, bruised, despised, smitten and rebuked. All he endured on our behalf for he so loved us. He endured unto death, even the death on the cross. The death on cross is said to be the fiercest or brutal death to be experienced. "Let us therefore come boldly to the throne of grace, that we may obtain mercy and grace to help in time of need" (Hebrew 4:16). We are called to rejoice when we become part takers of the sufferings of Jesus Christ. When our attitude towards sufferings is transformed through our faith in Jesus, the enduring grace will take over our sufferings and enable us to rejoice so that we will be glorified along with Jesus Christ. God our father wants to seat us also beside him where His son is seated. So, the sufferings of this present time are not worthy to be compared with the glory awaiting us. If we can believe these words of consolation, we will comprehend the concept of enduring grace.

Apostle Paul when he was writing to Timothy, persecution of Christians was widespread. Many of his followers had left him and some even deserted Christ. In such an environment Paul exhorts Timothy, "So you, my child be strong in the grace that is in Christ Jesus". Paul experienced it and hence he can encourage Timothy and us to enjoy this enduring grace in faith. Because the world we live is not favoring the way of Jesus, it is antagonistic towards Christian faith, we have to be strong in the Lord and his grace to face any attacks from our adversaries. Paul compares an enduring Christian to a soldier, an athlete and a farmer who are faithful in their calling enduring all difficulties to accomplish their goal. Yes, endurance has a result. In Romans 5:1-4 we see that tribulations works patience, patience experience or otherwise steadfastness and steadfastness hope. Hope is of the glory of God in which is our rejoicing. Our assurance of salvation is where our hope meets with the will of God about us. Being justified by faith when we enjoy peace with God through Jesus Christ we are blessed with the grace of God. Grace produces various virtues in us on experiencing endurance. Endurance we can say is the identity or the hallmark of a true Christian.

To receive God's promises we need patience (Hebrew 10:36). God had spoken through Isaiah "thus saith the Lord, the Holy One of Israel, and his maker, ask me of things to come concerning my sons, and concerning the work of my hands command ye me".

(45:11 KJV). That is the relationship with God we are invited to enter through Jesus Christ and as partakers of his sufferings. The promise is of having authority over all the works of his hand. If this is given to Israel how much more is the privileges of his children redeemed through the blood of His only begotten son. James refers to the prophets of the Lord who suffered afflictions and experienced endurance as examples for the believers specifically pointing out the patience of Job. James establishes that their patience and endurance made them blessed. Also, we see Jeremiah being strengthened by the Lord before being sent to the people of Israel.'Behold, I have made thee this day a defensed city, and an iron pillar, and brazen walls against the whole land, against the kings of Judah, against the princes there of, against the priests thereof and against the people of the land' (1:17-18). The eyes of God are on us. Unless he provides us with sufficient strength, he will not cause us to face sufferings. It is our unbelief and lack of trust in God that make us weary in the face of sufferings. We shall be steadfast in our faith to enjoy the grace of endurance. Our foundation shall be on Jesus Christ our savior. 'The Lord is faithful, who shall stablish you and keep you from evil' (2 Thessalonians 3:3).

We have already seen that we are adopted to be the children of God and hence we are eligible for the delightful, goodly, and wonderful inheritance in the kingdom. This eligibility for inheritance also brings in its train reasonable disciplinary procedures also- "…for whom the lord loveth, he chastens and scourges every son he receives…. But if he be without chastisement, whereof all are partakers, then are ye bastards and not sons" (Hebrews 12: 6, 8). The Psalmist prays to the lord "…search me…and test me…". His punishments are warnings for us and His warnings are his acts of grace. God is slow to anger and rich in love. (Psalms 145:8).

> *"At its heart, Enduring Grace is a living testament to how we can make peace with sorrow and disappointment and bring joy and transcendence into our lives" Quote*

In my life when I was tested to the extent of questioning God for the pain I suffered. I had to suffer severe pain in my legs for about four years continuously without sleep in the nights. My wife also became weak taking care of me and massaging my legs during sleepless nights and helping me in my routine chores as I was bedridden. My mother who was around ninety and always in bed, after having treated for cardiac problems, was also attended by my wife Sisy. Even though a maid was appointed for her, her care was insufficient. Already I am under medication for diabetes and Leukemia (CML) and is under continued medical surveillance. During the sleepless nights, I spent long hours in prayer, but I doubted whether God turned his ears away from me. My relatives, church members and friends and many who even do not know me personally were all praying for me. During this period God strengthened me to study the Bible more curiously to understand His ways and His will for me. As the Psalmist said it "It is good for me that I have been afflicted; that I might learn thy statutes" (Psalms 119:71). Doctors could not diagnose my problem after all possible tests used in neurology including nerve biopsy. Observing the symptoms, they named my illness as Mono Neuritis Multiplex (MNM). But no solution for it because the cause of it could not be detected. Hence, they could not prescribe proper medicine other than certain pain killers used in neurological problems which I have been taking for the previous four years. God's grace enabled me to endure the suffering. Now after two more years I can walk without help even if with a little difficulty. Pain is almost relieved. The Israelites could start their journey only when the cloud lifted from above the tabernacle. Otherwise, they Would have to wait in their camp till the day when the cloud lifted (Exodus 40:36). There are periods in the lives of God's children when the cloud remains on them as they wait for the will of God . All these physical ailments started working in me when I decided to quit my job and start missionary and charitable work among the downtrodden and tribal people. God tests in many ways. We are not expected to question

God's authority over us because he has bought us for a great ransom, and we are his own. Trials, tribulations, and hardships may be the form of testing. Such experiences make us perfect, strong, more patient and steadfast in our hope (Romans 5: 2- 4; 1 Peter 5: 10). "All things God works for the good of those who love Him". God uses trials and tribulations to generate spiritual power in His elect ones. It is grace that makes us withstand such pressures. Are we strengthened, empowered, and emboldened through tribulations and trials? If so, we are enjoying the grace of God and He is the God of all graces.

God sends his disciplinary actions time and again for all humans to repent and obey his words and rejoice in the salvation He offered to the world. It is his patience and endurance on human beings that the people of this world are not so far destroyed. We see in the OT period that he sent destruction whenever the wretchedness of the people consumed the land. God is giving us time to repent." The Lord is gracious and compassionate, slow to anger and rich in love. The Lord is good to all; He has compassion on all He has made" (Psalms 145: 8-9).

Sharing Grace

We may be sympathetic at times, but are we empathetic and willing to share the benefits of grace with others? Are we still brooding over engrossed in our worldly riches claiming them to be the grace of God? I think we are miserably mistaken. Jesus taught us to clothe naked, feed the hungry and so on. He told the young man who came seeking the way to the heavenly kingdom to sell and distribute his wealth to the needy. If we can do that without persuasion, spontaneously, then we can say that we are living in grace. What is our response towards the divine grace which is the sacrificial love of God towards us? Is our life influenced by this sacrificial grace? Jesus at the last supper shared his flesh and blood with the disciples and set an example to be followed. Our attitude for sharing marks the evidence of God's grace in us. God wants us to be rich in doing good works (Titus 3:1,8,14.) Are we still considering the worldly riches the grace of God? Has our attitude changed to that of Paul as seen in Philipians 3:7-8 - to count as loss those things which we consider as gain in this world? If we are not merciful to others we will be judged without mercy (James 2:13). Mercy is one of the adttributes of the fruit of grace. 'Then shall the king say unto them on his right hand; come ye blessed of my father, inherit the kingdom prepared for you from the foundation of the world: For I was hungered, and ye gave me meat; I was thirsty and ye gave me drink, I was a stranger, and ye took me in; naked and ye clothed me; I was in prison and ye came unto me .... verily I say unto you, in as much as you have done it unto one of the least of these my brethren, ye have done it unto me' (Matthew 25:34-40).

Forgiving Grace

We can claim to be in God's grace only if we can reflect the grace of forgiveness like a mirror. (2 Corinthians 3: 18). Otherwise, our claim is meaningless. God forgives all our sins and transgressions, we believe. We are justified freely by His grace through the redemption that is in Christ Jesus. Moreover, He has promised that our sins will not be remembered anymore. So, we also have to be kind and forgiving one another (Ephesians 4:32, Matthew 6:14-15}. 'Are we transformed by the renewing of our mind'. The forgiving grace we can enjoy only if we are reconciled to God our heavenly father. Grace abounds only in His presence. There is happiness and rejoicing, fulness of happiness only in the presence of divine grace in us. We read God's forgiving grace in Matthew 18: 32- 35. The debtor who got his debts written off could not show mercy to the

> *The assurance of heaven is never given to the person. And that is why at the core of the Christian faith is the Grace of God. If there is one word I would grab from all of that, it's forgiveness – that you can be forgiven.*
> *– Ravi Zacharias*

person who owed him money. That fellow is seen punished for his behavior. Our confidence of having our sins forgiven is manifested only if we forgive others. Our acts of kindness are the expression of indwelling grace in us. It is our willingness to forgive that is reflecting God's glorious grace as through a mirror. Jesus taught his disciples to pray 'Forgive our debts as we forgive our debtors', this is for we too for praying not only an instruction to take into consideration while praying. Whatever we owe to do for others are all our debts. If we fail in fulfilling them, we agree that God may do to us likewise. It is only because God is merciful that we are not punished then and there. But we have to remember that we are accountable for even our words that hurt others in any manner. 'Forbearing one another, and forgiving one another, if any man has a quarrel against any; even as Christ forgave you, so do ye'. (Colossians 3:13). We have heard that " . to forgive is divine". We read in Matthew 18:21-22 how Jesus responded to the question of Peter about how many times a person shall forgive. Grace is not a matter for quantification rather it shall flow ceaselessly as God's grace is eternal on us.

Empowering Grace

In the OT periods God reveals His might when the Israelites were encountered with difficult situations. We see kings and prophets lamenting for the interference of God to save them. Many people are given strength to defeat the enemies of Israel. Israel the nation was of concern to God. When we come to the New Testament, it is observed that the covenant is established with individuals who are saved through faith. The obligations of the first part which is of God is already accomplished. Those who come under the agreement accepting the offer and fulfilling its terms through Jesus Christ are entitled to enjoy the benefits of the covenant. Spiritual and physical empowerment *inter alia* is a benefit offered through this covenant. Why we feel on certain occasions that we are weak and cannot withstand the attacks of our adversary is only because of our unawareness of Him who promised to be with us in any situations. Elisha's servant could see the horses and chariots of fire when his eyes the Lord opened. It is said about the musk deer that it wanders here and there in search of the smell without knowing that itself is the source of the smell. Likewise, we too without discerning the power bank we have in us become weary and feel groaning.

'His divine power has given us everything we need for a godly life through our knowledge of him who called us by his own glory and goodness.' (2 Peter 1:3). We can see in the Bible how this great power acted through many a saint. Bible is full of such stories. The power acting through humans is immeasurable as the power source is unimaginable! Jesus' discourse with his disciples also reveal that everything is possible with all who believe. So, the knowledge of him who promised such powers to the believer is necessary to experience that superpower. Knowledge here does not refer to just information and understanding rather the understanding and living with that understanding. That we may call wisdom, knowledge in action or faith in action.

'He gives power to the faint; and to them that have no might He increases strength' (Isaiah 40:29). God cannot change his nature and character. He is the same yesterday, today and forever. 'Come to me, all you who are weary and burdened, and I will give you rest'. (Matthew 11:28). He empowers all who trust Him in his promises.

Once Jesus said to Paul "my grace is sufficient for you," Paul is satisfied with it. He accepted it as such and in every suffering, he endured without grumbling or mistrusting God. He states that God comforts them in every tribulation. Further he says, "for as the sufferings of Jesus abound in us, so our consolation also abounds by Christ." This is the effect of experiencing God's empowering grace. Jesus promised even the power to blow up a mountain. When the divine grace works in us, we will not see mountains in our ways. It may be mountain for non-believers. What we see is the face of our

Lord in all our situations. In 2 Kings 6 there is the episode of the servant of Elisha beholding a host of horses and chariots sent by the king of Syria to catch Elisha. But when his eyes was opened by the Lord, he could see the mountain filled with horses and chariots of fire around Elisha. Here we see the difference between the outlook of a man of God and a man of this world. That is the experience of grace. 'Though he was crucified through weakness, yet he lives by the power of God. For we also are weak in him, but we shall live with him by the power of God toward you'. (2 Corinthians 13:4). How great is the Christian experience of living with divine powers and bearing fruits of the spirit? We are not our own. We are purchased by God for a great ransom, the blood of his only begotten son and we are to live for the purpose of our owner. As he has also adopted us as his children, we are to serve him as true children. The Old Testament people were given abundant material benefits as blessings and physical powers to win over their enemies. When we come to the New Testament, our enemies are not from this world and our treasures are not of this world. It is grace that leads us victoriously in this world with the power to overcome temptations and all satanic attacks and increasing our treasures in the heavenly places with our good deeds in this world. Love of this world is enmity with God. When Stephen was stoned "... he kneeled down and cried with a loud voice, Lord, lay not this sin to their charge". A true live illustration for God's empowering grace. Paul and all other disciples, and many bishops of early churches, many true believers embraced martyrdom experiencing the empowering grace of God. Paul advises Timothy, "But watch thou in all things, endure afflictions, do the work of an evangelist, make full proof of thy ministry". We may be doing the ministry of God or doing the work of evangelists, are we mentally ready to endure afflictions in our ways. In many countries, spreading gospel is forbidden even though not by law but by many local people of other religions. Do we have the perseverance to pray for them or are we moving against them through legal proceedings? Do we exhibit the full proof of our ministry? If we fail in these areas, we are not yet experiencing the power of grace. We must submit ourselves before our Lord Jesus Christ so that his power may rest upon us. Then we can emphatically declare that when I am weak, then am I strong. His grace is sufficient for me, for my strength is made perfect in weakness.

We know the life and experience of many OT people in their assignment of leading the nation, Israel. The prayers of Jehoshaphat and Asa are all-time prayers for Christians. " …. For we have no power to face this vast army that is attacking us. We do not know what to do, but our eyes are on you, Lord there is no one like you to help the powerless against the mighty ……. do not let mere mortals prevail against you". The level of spiritual strength exhibited by Elijah is also available even in many folds for us today. We need to show the same level of faith to experience that power. For example, we are not or cannot be a source of the power, but we can utilize power within our control as a sail is used in the ship in stormy weather or electricity is used for our equipment. We also have to accept and admit that our power is nothing, and seek God, the power source in every walk of our life for his empowering grace. Our prayer in faith can also bring down a gracious dew or melting fire as Elijah could do empowered by the spirit of God. But what we have to understand is that the promises and the way of dealings of God are different for the OT and NT peoples, but His nature cannot be changed. We are more blessed than the OT people because God gave us direct access towards Him through Jesus Christ who is the mediator of the new covenant. ' …. Thanks be to God, who always leads us as captives in Christ's triumphal procession and uses us to spread the aroma of the knowledge of him everywhere' (2 Corinthians 2:14). We are victors everywhere and in anything and our power is to be used for the glory of God. Empowering grace makes us triumph over our adversary. "Our fight is not against flesh and blood, but against the authorities, against the powers of this dark world and against the spiritual forces of evil in the heavenly realms" (Ephesians 6:12). Also, the psalmist stated, and Paul reinstated that God made man in his image and has put all things under his authority." Let us therefore come boldly unto the throne of grace, that we may obtain mercy, and find grace to help in time of need" (Hebrews 4:16). That is why we name our times as the age of grace. This period may end unawares at any time.

Never Ending Grace

We call the son of that man in Luke 15 'Prodigal Son'. We call him wasteful, extravagant, irresponsible and all the bad words we can see in the dictionary. Shall we be justified in referring him with such words?

Let us come to the story of the so-called prodigal son. He leaves his father's house, amassing all the material wealth he can claim from his father. He leaves the house with the material wealth only. His *sonship* does not get lost by his leaving. But he rejects the authority of his father then onwards. But the father does not reject his love towards the son. He is always the graceful father, and his grace never ends. When that person came to his senses, he came back to his father's house. The picturization of the scene would be quite emotional and heartbreaking. There we see the awesome grace of compassion spurting from the heart of a father. He didn't fail to recognize his son though he might have come in a shabby or starved appearance. The compassionate father didn't wait to question him for his misbehavior before extending his hands of love to hold him to his heart in an embrace. If an earthly father treats his prodigal son in this way how much more can we expect from our heavenly father who adopted us knowing our nature. Our heavenly father purchased us from the possession of the evil one not by paying in silver, gold, or such perishable things, but by the blood of his only son. His grace will never fade away from us or he will never leave us even if we reject his claim over us. So great a ransom He has paid for us. – for what? To praise his *glorious grace* throughout our life! Do we have a compassionate heart? If the answer is yes, then we can claim that the grace of God dwells in us.

Here is a point to ponder. The son on leaving his father's house had spent his wealth according to his will. He could have even invested in a business and earned more wealth. If that had happened most Christians would say, "by the grace of God, he is well settled". The relationship and love between father and son are not at all a matter of concern even among believers now-a-days. Now we can see a generation among traditional Christians who claim they are blessed because of their ancestral wealth and tradition. But they do not care to remember a past generation who struggled too hard and persevered persecutions in their endeavor to spread the gospel of the Kingdom. Their hope was in the heavenly treasures. As King Solomon was blessed with all wisdom as he prayed for and additionally given all worldly wealth, these blessed forefathers were bestowed with honor and wealth in the next generations. Some among those new generations praise the lord for his grace whereas some others enjoy the world forgetting the source of their blessings. Still, they claim it is the grace of God. Do this worldly wealth and possession amount to God's grace? Our forefathers enjoyed true grace when they were tormented or afflicted for the sake of the kingdom of God. We have become the benefactors of God's grace towards them. It is, in a sense, only the *fringe benefits* which the almighty God promised along with his son Jesus when he was given in sacrifice for our countless sins. Heavenly blessing, which is the divine grace is available only to those who search for His kingdom and righteousness. The benefits, even though material, amount to grace only if we acknowledge that it is given along with the joy of salvation through the blood of Jesus Christ. Otherwise, it is only the mercy and kindness that God gives to all humans, good or evil. It is high time we are snatched by our nape and brought to our senses by some forces. It is grace only that does this wonderful work on us. Paul says – God's grace is sufficient for him, for His strength is made perfect in weakness. - whatever be the situation (2 Corinthians 12:9).

Conclusion

Let me conclude by just referring to the Old Testament book Exodus 25. There we see God's direction to Moses about the construction of the tabernacle. We see many things inside the ark of testimony. There is the golden censer representing worship, the pot with manna that represents God's provision, the rod of Aaron that budded which represents God's election and the miracles of God, the tables of covenant etc. But above all we see the mercy seat which as per the New Testament we may change to grace seat of God on which God reveals himself to the people. Without the grace seat or the presence of God in the sanctuary what meaning is there for all those other things whether it is worldly possessions, miracles, worship, or proclamation of the word of God.? The mercy seat that is to find a place in our person, which is the temple of God, should make us manifest mercy, kindness, and love towards others, if not we are mere hypocrites and God's grace does not abide in us. We see the description of the sanctuary in Hebrews 9: 1- 5 also. We are supposed to be the abode of our Lord. Let us introspect and see whether we conform to the sanctuary according to the will of God. Do we truly have a seat of grace above all other things, in our heart – a holiest place where the Lord will manifest? '*.. know ye not that your body is the temple of the holy ghost which is in you, which ye have of God, and ye are not your own? For ye are bought with a price, therefore, glorify God in your body and in your spirit, which are God's'* (1 Corinthians 6:19, 20). "Salvation is free, but not cheap". So, grace is the precious gift that God gave us through our Lord Jesus Christ. Jesus Christ has chosen us in Him before the foundation of the world for the praise of the glory of His grace.

3

Are You in Faith...?

Apostle St.Paul's letters to various churches are considered as the basics of Christian theology. Each epistle deals with profound spiritual subjects in Christian life and thought among all categories of peoples – Jews and gentiles. The subjects are relevant in the first century as well as the present. Here I wish to enlarge in brief on the core of faith based on a question tossed to the Corinthians. What is the relevance of the captioned question and instruction to test themselves given by Paul to the church towards the end of his second letter even when he had addressed them as holy and sanctified people? (2 Corinthians 13:5)

"Are you a believer?" is a question often asked by certain group of Christians to every other person whom they come across, who belong to other church groups. I think even the person who questions, and others may not be aware of the true meaning of the question, or the depth of the subject. Definitions for the word 'faith' are umpteen based on biblical verses and concepts formulated from the life experience of many of the forefathers of faith. I could once attend a Christian prayer meeting, a friend and relative of mine invited me to attend. Everything went on well and fine till a subject for prayer was put forth by one of the members. The leading pastor asked everyone to stand in a circle, holding the hands forming a chain and pray together for the cause of that person. The prayer gained momentum and voices turned out to be screams and screeches. The paster was shouting believe…, believe…, believe … incessantly, keeping his hands on the "seeker of blessing". I wonder if one can acquire belief if somebody pressurize you to believe. We all say, we are in Christian faith, or we believe in Jesus Christ, we are Christian believers. If nothing happens when we pray, we comfort ourselves saying that it is not God's will for us. Are we truly convinced or satisfied in our Christian faith? Are we committed to our faith as is envisaged in the Bible? Have we ever thought whether God our father is satisfied in our faith or are we comfortable or self-satisfied in our faith?

> *The law of the Christian life is ever, 'according to your faith be it unto you'; 'believe that ye receive and ye have them.' So then the more faith a man exercises the more of God and Christ he has.*

Jesus said to Martha "you will see the glory of God if you believe". She believed Jesus and she had already affirmed her belief saying that if he were there her brother would not have died. She also believed that Lazar will resurrect at the final call. Her faith seems to be limited. She is seen as a practical hostess engrossed in many things physically and of course may also be mentally. Her faith was footed on her practical experiences. Is our faith like that of Martha? What is the level of faith we are expected to exhibit in our lives ?

Faith

Belief, trust, and faith are defined by many persons in different ways and these words are often interchanged. When there germinates some idea in our mind occasionally from what we hear or see it remains there just as a thought, and we tend to ponder over it. Later on, when we get a proof of its existence, we begin to believe it. We accept that such things exist. Further when we experience benefits of certain things, we start trusting it for our future conducts and in our needs of life. It is true about persons in our contacts and other things animate or inanimate. So far, the progress is based on evidence, proofs, reasonings and logics. There after our conduct is based on those acquired understandings which we accept as our belief.

Faith is a noun. Faith is even more supposed to be religious in its entirety. The strength and level of a Christian's faith determines his character and credibility. Being in faith, we feel a consciousness of its need, a strong desire and a confident expectation. It emerges from our innermost heart. As the Psalmist says, 'As the deer pants for the streams of water.' A great unquenched thirst is experienced to merge with God in faith. It gives an assurance getting unto what we have not yet seen or heard of as the author of Hebrews puts it. Hebrews 11:1 says faith is being sure of what we hope for and certain of what we do not see. Here we can see that faith is the crux or core substance of hope which leads our life to a certain goal. It is self-denial and complete dependence on, or harmonizing with God, precisely the opposite of a self-dependent isolation which shuns us away from God.

Measure of Faith

When we study the book of Romans, Paul says in chapter 12 about a measure of faith that God has allotted to every man. So, we may say that faith is also a measure of the capacity to receive gifts from God. This measure we receive first when we accept Jesus Christ as our redeemer and Savior. And benchmark capacity is the abiding of the Holy Spirit in us (Romans 8:23). That measure is the same for each person.' There are different kinds of gifts, but the same spirit' … 'there are different kinds of working, but in all of them and in everyone it is the same God at work' …. 'All these are the work of one and the same spirit' (1 Corinthians 12: 4-11). This forms the foundation on which we must build our faith life receiving further gifts in abundance. Christian faith is dynamic till eternity, and not static. The intensity of our faith shall increase (2 Peter 1:3-11). The measure of grace was given to each one of us according to the gift of Christ (Ephesians 4:7). We receive the gifts according to the measure that God wills, and we use the gifts according to the assignment given to us based also on the other parameters defining our capacity. Everything is provided by the divine will. It is clearly illustrated in Romans, God's word and letting his truth become the catalyst of our faith. This is the message we see in the story Jesus said about the person allocating talents to his servants. The measure of talent differs but the level of trust and faith the master expected from his servants is the same. The profit expected is proportional to what is given to them and not more. Master knows their capacity to deal with the talent. God is satisfied with our contribution for His Kingdom if we faithfully do His will with what we are given. When we do this, then we will be able to test and prove his perfect will for us (Romans 12:2). Our actions then will be in unison with the will of God, and we will reflect the image of Jesus in our lives.

Do we have the attitude to know the will of God and surrender to it? How can we know the will of the Father? We must know the will of the Father because only those who do the will of the Father can enter into the Kingdom of God (Matthew 7:21). For that we must repent and surrender that old serpent seed which is doing our will that is of flesh, which is against the Father's will. Repentance means, surrender to Him, and do His will from this time on. The *Will* of the Father that cannot be known by man of flesh will be known by His children because they will be written in their *hearts and in their minds*. They will be lifted from the hold of written word, the law written on tablets to become the *Living Word implanted in our spirit*, in our minds and in our hearts. The Father's will, will automatically become our life, just as the serpent seed had become our life when we were born in the flesh. The sin that deprives us from knowing the will of God was really a trespasser in our life. It is faith in God that enables and empowers us to oust the trespasser from our domain. This we call regeneration or rebirth in the spirit – becoming a new creature. The full measure of faith is the end factor that works in us to achieve the salvation of our souls (1 Peter 1:9).

Faith as a Possession and Divine gift.

So often this has been pitted against each other as contradictory when in reality they are complementary. ***'It is He that worketh in us both to will and to do of His own good pleasure'***. The great and precious gift God has extended to us is His son Jesus Christ 'set forth, crucified' among us (Galatians 3:1). The condition given is 'receive' and 'believe' Him (John 1:12). No more reference is required to explain how faith becomes a gift and a possession both at the same time. It is our part to receive the gift when it is offered. No gift is forcefully invested on us.

We shall take stock of the loaves that we have, and put them in His hands, that He may give them back to us so multiplied as to be more than adequate to the needs of the thousands. When we submit our body as a sacrifice, living and holy and pleasing to God as clean vessel, He will fill us with the Holy Spirit and divine strength which is the gift. Then we say *we have this treasure in jars of clay* to show that this all-surpassing power is from God and not from us. This treasure is the *'most holy faith'* described by Apostle Jude. By the surrender of our self and the renewal of our mind comes the realization that we have been given the gift of the precious faith just as all the saints before us received (2 Peter 1:1). To receive the gift, we must extend our heart towards God as an honorable and clean vessel. This gift of faith which is the Holy Spirit itself we must hold on as our most valuable possession as a Christian. Our faith is the tool for making ourselves qualified to receive abundant gifts. The offer of His only begotten Son on the cross, our acceptance and belief of Jesus Christ as the only way for our salvation contributes to our life of faith and qualifies us for further abundant spiritual gifts. Paul says in 1 Corinthians 2:12 'What we have received is not the spirit of the world, but the spirit who is from God, that we may understand what God has freely given us'. This is what happens to a man who is in faith. It is very easily said, but how it is to be achieved or possessed remains a mystery for many Christians. It is easy to be spoken of vociferously, rhetorically, and emotionally, but without the power, as envisaged in the gospel. The only way to be in faith is the complete surrender of our self or ego. The Holy Spirit takes the place of human spirit and sustains us in faith.

There seems to be some confusion with many Christians about the fact that salvation is the gift of God, and we don't have to work for it and the statement that' we are saved by faith· The statements are true to the extent of physical works that are the rites and customs and works of the Law· But some mental and spiritual exercises need to be done in this regard from our part. That is to open the door of our hearts, to receive Jesus who always keeps knocking at the door, and keep the vessel of clay, our body and mind clean to receive the gift of Holy Spirit.

Is it Practical to Live in Faith?

When it comes to faith it is generally considered devoid of reasoning, logic, evidence, or proof. Somebody is heard to have illustrated faith as "chicken gravy without seeing chicken bones. Faith requires no evidence for belief nor practice. The very nature of faith surmises that tangible evidence doesn't exist." We just accept it as a character or part of our individuality, and we possess it and keep it as one of our traits. We hold on to it strongly safeguarding it as a precious possession. A Christian of faith will walk the talk with Christian identity. The name of our faith, Christianity, symbolizes our identity with Christ and not just the name of a religion. I have heard of a believer having taught the children of the Sunday school that it is not hundred percent practical to live a Christian life as per the Bible! That teacher said it according to her life experience, but many Christians are leading their life in a fifty-fifty manner. Why does this happens? It is because of our doubt about the possibility of things happening according to our faith. We are doubtful about the prayers we make before God of whether it is according to God's will or self- will. We quite often ignore the promises given in the New Testament and hold on to the promises of material things promised to the nation of Israel. We still want Jesus to convert water to vine for us rather than wanting to transform us to a new creature. We want God to protect us from being pelted by others rather than seeing the heavenly glory when pelted as Stephen had seen. We are least interested to 'be found in Him, not having mine own righteousness, which is of the law but that which is through the faith of Christ, the righteousness which is of God by faith' (Philippians 3:9). If we are to enjoy the power of the Spirit and power of his resurrection in our life we must live in true faith, that enables us to suffer and conform to the death of Christ. Hence, the enabling grace works in us to lead a Christian faith life. Enoch, Noah, Abraham, Moses, Joshua, Caleb etc., persons in Bible; the sacrifice of Abraham, Ark of Noah, events during the journey of Israelites, Jericho etc.; Paul and many other saints in New Testament, are all solid historic proof and evidence for any person to believe in the Bible and have faith in Jesus Christ. For those who are vehement on proof and evidence of a living God the history of Israel will suffice.

Levels of Faith

From our birth onwards during our growth and development, our thoughts are formed and influenced by our observations through our senses, our learning, experiences in life etc. There is progress in our capacity to assimilate things as we grow. This process we call as the development of human individuality. We develop various faculties during our growth. We get during this course, information, and experiences regarding the things in this universe and beyond. We develop the knowledge of extra-terrestrials, and we try to convert it to concepts after analyzing it with available information, reasoning, and logic. Similarly, the seed of spiritual thinking is also sown in our minds.

We develop a concept for our belief and trust based on various outside resources. When it comes to faith we rely on our own conviction and discard the other sources of information and evidence. The understanding based on the observations of the material world which is purely connected with our body and senses including emotional triggers, forms the first stage of growth. Then starts learning for acquisition of knowledge and it forms the second stage along with the first and takes on as intellectual development. Here we employ information reason and logic to understand things around in our lives. Most people live in these two stages and end up ignoring the third and most important part of our personality, the Spirit. We know that personality is the combination of body, soul, and spirit. Human being is not perfected without spirit which is the pinnacle of the beingness of man. Jesus said 'I have spoken to you of earthly things, and you do not believe, how then will you believe if I speak of heavenly things' (John 3:12). Hence the development towards heavenly things shall begin with the knowledge and understanding of earthly things. God gives us a chance to understand him through various means of His manifestations in this universe, our families, opportunities to learn from people around us, through our studies, our churches and many other medias and our own experiences of the super naturals. Also, he has given us the freedom to choose either life or death. We may direct our studies either to accept or reject the spiritual things. And likewise, we can possess faith too through different means God has provided for us in this world.

Only when we reach the maturity to think of the futility of things in this world based on our life experiences and intellectual development will we start to think of transcendental matters. We no more depend on logic or reasoning which is required only to establish material or physical things. We become aware of things which are beyond human perceptions. The discourse between Elihu and Job (Book of Job) is an example of a debate for and against the material and the metaphysical. Elihu and the three others spoke from their knowledge (intellect) of God and nothing wrong about God is spoken by them, but Job talked from his experience of God (a confident conviction in his spirit). Likewise, knowledge of God need not amount to living in faith with God. Knowing God is to know him according to His glory, according to the works of His hands, accordingly as he has revealed himself in this universe and His salvific works for the humanity. To possess such understanding of God and faith in God, the so far acquired knowledge and intelligence of and about God the Father, Jesus the Son and the Holy Spirit, we must transfer them from our head to our hearts. The story of the Samaritan woman explains it. When the people from the town come in a personal relationship with Jesus, they testify that now we believe not because of your words but because we ourselves are convinced. Even when we say we are believers, if our love for God is not spurting from our heart, faith is a farce. The Israelites who were redeemed from the slavery of Pharaohs lived in the desert forty years. They didn't have to toil daily for their livelihood. Every day supply came from above. Their job was to collect and eat as they wished. There too they grumbled and complained. That is the real state of many Christians while they claim to be saved by the blood of Jesus. It resembles the Israelites in the wilderness. 1 Corinthians 10:1-11 is given as reference for us and strongly says this is an example for us. Yes, an example to understand that just declaring that "I am born again" does not make us qualified for the Kingdom of God. If we are living the wilderness life, we are still men of flesh who cannot even discern the things above. Only when we cross the Jordan, that is the experience of becoming the spiritual man, we get transformed in the likeness of Jesus Christ. We become one with God. There we must face Jericho, we have to fight the enemies, we have to toil hard, all to keep us steadfast in faith. The "outside-in" life gets translated to an "inside-out" life. Then, we will say in agreement with Paul 'I have fought the good fight, I have finished my course, I have kept the faith: henceforth there is laid up for me a crown of righteousness. ….'. This is faith life.

When we grow in faith our thoughts are stirred up by divine intuitions from above. Then our all activities are motivated by spirit and not by flesh. Our mind gives way to the mind of God.

Many believers often confuse having faith in God with believing in God. Many people "believe" Jesus Christ really exists. Many believe he is who he claimed to be – God himself and the Savior of the world. But that only is not faith. That's just mental assent. An acceptance of the facts. The Bible says demons too "believe" in this way (James 2:19).

Biblical faith is very different. More than 60 times, the New Testament tells us eternal life is given to those who put their faith in Christ alone for salvation. Nelson's Bible Dictionary defines faith as a belief in or confident attitude toward God, involving *commitment to his will for one's life*. Nelson also says belief is to place one's trust in God's truth. A person who believes is one who takes God at his word and trusts in him for salvation.

> *Biblical faith goes beyond mental acceptance of the facts. Biblical faith is like actually buying an air ticket like fastening your seat belt and trusting that pilot to take you up and back down again. Biblical faith is trust – putting your eternal destiny in the hands of this Jesus who claims to be the only savior of the world.*

Either we are convinced by the facts of life, the facts of our background, education or even the facts about what we know about God.

Faith is a noun. It is something you have, or you possess, as your own and using or enjoying it, safeguarding and depending on it for your complete satisfaction. Faith in God is the confident belief that He is very personal to me. We know faith as a very personal relationship from the attitude of Mary Magdalene (John 20:11-15). She supposing the man behind her as the gardener said, '...... Sir, if thou hast borne him, hence, tell me where thou hast laid him, and I will take him away.' True faith reveals true love. Rather than universalizing God as the sovereign Creator of all things and that He can and will do anything according to His will, we shall accept and acknowledge him as a personal possession always abiding in and with us making our life worthy for him. As Paul said, 'everything is possible for me through Him who strengthens me'. Trust, on the other hand, is a verb. It is something you do or act upon. It comes into play when you are in action for the accomplishment of your activity. Faith always comes first, but trust is never guaranteed. When our trust is acted upon earnestly and honestly expecting its result as assured then trust becomes faith. (Mark 11:24)

There are many in the world who cannot accept things that are not proved scientifically. Even so-called Christians are hesitant to accept divine interference in the life of holy people. Most people may not understand the power of faith. Faith imparts to the believer empowering and enabling grace. We know that the seekers of evidence and proof for everything in this universe could reach nowhere in their searches. Many things they have searched out is already written in the word of God. More than that Bible is the perfect prospectus that deals with offers and promises to the life course of a man in this life to finish the course successfully. Isaiah 34:16 says '…. seek ye out of the book of the Lord, and read; no one of these shall fail, none shall lack her mate, ….'. Which means none of the prophesies there in or what is written therein shall remain unaccomplished. So, it is good to make things confirmed through research too.

God asks Job certain questions.

Job 38:4 Where wast thou when I laid the foundations of the earth? declare, if thou hast understanding.

38:5 Who hath laid the measures thereof, if thou knowest? or who hath stretched the line upon it?

38:6 Whereupon are the foundations thereof fastened? or who laid the corner stone thereof;

38:7 When the morning stars sang together, and all the sons of God shouted for joy?

38:8 Or who shut up the sea with doors, when it brakes forth, as if it had issued out of the womb? .... The answer to these questions we see in 42:3-4. 'Who is he that hideth counsel without knowledge? therefore have I uttered that I understood not: things too wonderful for me, which I knew not. .... I will demand of thee and declare thou unto me.' Faith and fear and love of God give us knowledge and wisdom. 'Those who think they know something do not yet know as they ought to know (1 Corinthians 8:2)'.

We now see scientists seeking the origin of the universe and creations. They could not reach at a strong evidence or proof. They are still putting on assumptions. Atheists may hold upon it as logic. This logic will take you nowhere as it gives way to other questions which cannot be answered reasonably. So, it is logical and reasonable to understand things spiritually that provides us with knowledge surpassing all human understandings. Here we need true faith to discern divine wisdom. So, letting our minds think of things above will lead us to eternal life, peace, and happiness. Among Christians we see three types of faith that can be named as: -

- Emotional faith
- Intellectual faith and
- Spiritual or Salvific Faith.

> *Faith is different from proof; the latter is human; the former is a Gift from God.*
> *- Blaise Pascal*

Let us analyze the life of three persons in the Bible to understand the nature of different types of faith and compare our faith.

1. The young, rich man who came to Jesus seeking eternal life.
2. The scribe who came asking which law is the greatest command. He is not far away from Kingdom of God.
3. Zacchaeus who attained salvation

We read the story of the young, rich man in Luke 18: 18-30. Now when Jesus heard these things, he said unto him, Yet lackest thou one thing: sell all that thou hast, and distribute unto the poor, and thou shalt have treasure in heaven: and come, follow me. When he heard this, he was very sad, as he was a very wealthy man. Jesus looked at him and said, 'How hard it is for the rich to enter the kingdom of heaven! Indeed, it is easier for a camel to go through the eye of a needle than for a rich man to enter into heaven'. The rich man is said to be lacking in one thing. But that one thing is everything that is needed to get access into the Kingdom of God. Leaving behind the world and longing for the eternal is the only one thing for a seeker of eternity to follow. We see Martha, as anxious and troubled about many things, Jesus said to her 'one thing is necessary, and Mary had chosen it'. Likewise, we may also be lacking in one thing that may shut the door of the Kingdom against us. We must identify what it is. Paul could deny everything that was once profitable to him when he came to live in Christ. He could declare that no more I am living for myself Christ is living in me. This we may call self- actualization, Human spirit becoming one with divine spirit. God expects nothing less from us than to be holy as He is holy. What is blocking us from this bonding. We must introspect our lives . For the rich, young man, the one thing he lacked was everything that denied his claim for the kingdom. Love of the world is enmity to God. The willingness to renounce everything we consider precious in our lives to achieve the most precious heavenly glory is what matters to make us one with God. The young man knows the Law, he claims to be observing the laws scrupulously, but not knowing the spirit of the Laws. He feels to be faithful to God according to his intellect. Such faith we may call *Intellectual Faith.*

The scribe who came asking Jesus which law is the greatest among laws is another example for intellectual faith. He too is not yet eligible for the Kingdom. Jesus says he is not far from the kingdom. Intellectual faith is believing based on knowledge and information and consistent with reasoning, logic, experience, and precedence. They harden their hearts against receiving the word of God in true spirit in their heart. About such people it is said by Paul in Ephesians 4:18 They are darkened in their understanding, alienated from the life of God because of the ignorance that is in them, due to their *hardness of heart.* And, in Romans 8:5-6 for they that are after the flesh do mind the things of the flesh; but they that are after the Spirit the things of the Spirit. For to be carnally minded is death; but to be spiritually minded is life and peace.

We usually pray quoting the power and strength of God revealed to our forefathers mentioned in the Bible. But many a time we are not confident that it can happen in our lives. That is because we are not sure about our salvation. Romans 10:9 That if thou shalt confess with thy mouth the Lord Jesus, and shalt believe in *thine heart* that God hath raised him from the dead, thou shalt be saved. So, what we believed through intelligence should *come down from brain to our heart.* The spirit of God then will abide in us and transform us to the likeness of Jesus. We will then reflect the image of Jesus in our lives. We too will be able to drink the cup that our father gives us. We will be able to do the will of God. When we are in faith, we will be faithful to God. Faithfulness is a vital ingredient or component in the fruit of Spirit and bearing fruit is *faith in action.* We see Paul's instruction to Timothy in chapter 2:2 'the things that you have heard of me among many witnesses, the same commit you to *faithful* men, who shall be able to teach others also'. It is required in stewards of the gospel (1 Corinthians 4:2). We must hold to the fundamentals of faith.

Zacchaeus' story is very different. He did not want Jesus or others to see him when he rushed to have a glance of Jesus. He just wanted to see how Jesus looks like. He was aware of his weakness. He was a man disliked by other Jews because of his occupation as tax collector for the Romans. He did not claim to have any lofty thoughts or ideals. He might have been driven by the talks in the society about Jesus. He also was just one among the common people who crowded to see a celebrity. He was triggered by the common man's emotion only. When Jesus called him by name from beneath the fig tree and disclosed his intention of staying that day with Zacchaeus, he hurried down. We see him starting to talk, before Jesus saying anything more to him. Luke 19: 6-10. So, he came down at once and welcomed him gladly. But Zacchaeus stood up and said to the Lord, 'Look, Lord! *Here and now,* I give half of my possessions to the poor, and if I have cheated anybody out of anything, I will pay back four times the amount'. There are quick reactions from him. He does not wait to consult his family or others or request for time to prepare his home. He received him in his *heart.* Reacting positively to the call of God. That made him qualified to be the son of Abraham. He was called son of Abraham not because of his heredity but because of his answering the call of God instantaneously in faith. The emotional thrust to join the crowd ended up in a spiritual stimulus to make drastic decisions in life. Even now we see Christians moving with the crowd making emotional spurts but lacking in stable or lasting spiritual effects. They are not driven to take decisions to give up their earthly tie-ups which hold them back in this world. Their emotional triggers last only up to the end of a spiritual meeting. We may call such faith as *emotional faith.* In the parable of the soil, the seeds fell on soils other than the good soil is the example for emotional believers. Their faith is not deep rooted, or root has not reached up to the heart. In Zacchaeus' case we see him surrendering his own self and all to the Lord. That we call faith - trust and surrender, - emotional faith being transferred to Spiritual faith.

As we surrender to the author and perfector of our faith, the Father's spiritual laws will be implanted within us – in our spirit, to become one with the Holy Spirit, in our mind and in our heart. We will experience everlasting peace and happiness when we become Kingdom citizens, sons, and daughters of the heavenly Father.

There was once a tight rope walker Blondin who could perform death defying feats without support or lifesaving equipment. Crowds gathered to watch his feats. He would walk across Niagara Falls over a tight rope. In an event, he performed the daring stunt and also took a wheelbarrow over the tight rope. He asked the audience ' Do you believe that I can take the wheelbarrow over the tight rope'. Everyone in the audience believed and cheered him. He said, 'In case you believe I can do it, who will sit on the wheelbarrow'. There were no volunteers.

Here we see that everyone had a firm belief that he could carry the wheelbarrow successfully over the tight rope. But no one wanted to volunteer to sit in the wheelbarrow and trust him with their lives. Here we see the difference between belief and trust or faith. All viewers have a belief that Blondin will do it successfully, but nobody wanted to trust him with their lives. Trusting with own self is faith.

Faith is a complete confidence in something we conceived, believed and fully trusted to make it our life. That means we cling to God with an obeying, submissive and purified heart. We cannot cling to God unless we become of the *same substance with God*. This is achieved by the spirit of God dwelling in us. 'Father and son will abide in him who loves Jesus and obeys' (John 14:23). We shall become the right and perfect stones that are suitable to be built on the foundation of Jesus Christ.

It is said that one man then volunteered to sit in the wheelbarrow. He was successfully carried to both sides in the wheelbarrow over the rope above the Niagara Falls. When he was asked how he could get the courage to volunteer for the task, he said, "He is my father and I know that he can do it." This is a message for all Christian believers to have faith in God our father, who can do everything for His children.

Jesus said, 'I am the vine, ye are the branches: He that abideth in me, and I in him, the same bringeth forth much fruit: for without me ye can do nothing (John 15:5)'. Paul could say 'I am crucified with Christ: nevertheless, I live; yet not I, but Christ liveth in me: and the life which I now live in the flesh I live by the faith of the Son of God, who loved me, and gave himself for me (Galatians 2:20)'. The experience of Paul reveals how one is translated into the image of Jesus through saving faith.

"Faith is the surrender of the mind, it's the surrender of reason, it's the only thing that makes us different from other animals. It's our need to believe and to surrender our skepticism and our reason, our yearning to discard that and put all our trust or faith in someone or something, that is the sinister thing to me. ... Out of all the virtues, all the supposed virtues, faith must be the most overrated." --Christopher Hitchens.

Trust in the LORD with all your heart and lean not on your own understanding." (Proverbs 3:5). Word of God is the tool to discern things as it is written in Hebrews 4:12 "For the word of God is quick and powerful, sharper than any two-edged sword, piercing even to the dividing asunder of soul and spirit, and of the joints and marrow and is a discerner of the thoughts and intents of the heart". It is very clear that we should learn to differentiate between spirit, soul (mind) and body and the thoughts arising thereof.

``*I could have no freedom in the thought of any other circumstances or business in life: All my desire was the conversion of the heathen, and all my hope was in God: God does not suffer me to please or comfort myself with hopes of seeing friends, returning to my dear acquaintance, and enjoying worldly comforts'.*`` --David Brainerd, a man of true faith, an American missionary who preached among Daleward Indians around New Jersey. (At the age of 27 on 7th October 1747 David died seriously affected with tuberculosis).

Peter says in   1 Peter 1:7, That the trial of your faith, being much more precious than of gold that perisheth, though it be tried with fire, might be found unto praise and honor and glory at the appearing of Jesus Christ: and in 2 Peter 5-8. And beside this, giving all diligence, add to your faith virtue; and to virtue knowledge; And to knowledge temperance; and to temperance patience; and to patience godliness; And to godliness brotherly kindness; and to brotherly kindness charity. For if these things be in you, and abound, they make you that ye shall neither be barren nor unfruitful in the knowledge of our Lord Jesus Christ

Emotionally or intellectually if we faithfully believe in the salvation through Jesus Christ, we are given the gift of the Holy Spirit. But for the Holy spirit to work in us we must allow Him. We must awaken Him lest we may perish. Our senses and, intellect are means of experiencing the surpassing knowledge of the divine.

I have experienced this in my life . When I was 9, I submitted myself to God accepting Jesus Christ as my redeemer and savior. May be an emotional act on my part, surely not an intellectual act. Afterwards during adolescence and youth, I used to pray and even speak in the parish without experiencing any spiritual urges within me. That was an intellectual performance only. I had lived according to my pleasure and desire just a common man ignoring the spirit of God in my youth. Even though I neglected the Holy Spirit, God did not allow me to perish or leave Him. I had become more and more involved in spiritual and gospel activities as the Holy Spirit directed me. I experienced His saving hands many times in the verge of death and accidents, His all-surpassing comforts and healing. I enjoyed where medical science rejected me as a case of no hope for survival. Then he gave me a great experience during a time of surviving on ventilator in 2004, May first week seriously affected by septicemia - I felt the presence of the Holy Spirit. My Lord didn't reject me. It was a miracle to the doctors who treated me, that a sudden change occurred in my physical conditions which they could not explain in medical terms. My Lord carried me through various trials to make me pure, holy, valuable and a useful weapon in his hands. I enjoy his love for me. Even when at times I become unfaithful to him he remains faithful in his precious promises.

Emotionally or intellectually if we accept Jesus Christ in our heart, I emphasize the word heart, we are safe in his hands. That means we must translate our emotional or intellectual faith to our heart to experience spiritual faith. If we then must pass through trials know that he wants our purification to be perfect. We must give up our peripheral emotive imitations of spiritual activities. Believe in truth and spirit, obey the word, fear the Lord with love and glorify Him in all our words and deeds in spontaneity from our heart. That is faith and let us be faithful to God and people we deal with. God bless us.

4

Assurance of Eternity

Most people even Christians are doubtful about their life after death. Is there such a thing as eternity? What could it be like? Can there be life after death by whatever name we call it, heaven, paradise, *moksha*, or anything of that kind? Christians vehemently advocate that there is life after death. They point their finger to two different realms of eternity as heaven and hell. There is no evidence even though there are many stories of rebirth. Gentiles may explain it as the rebirth of some other persons. Science tries to explain such things as psychic disorders of the kind of dissociative identity disorder or multiple personalities.

Jesus tells the story of a rich man and Lazarus picturizing Lazarus in the lap of Abraham and the rich man in trouble in the hells. The book of Revelations gives the picture of heaven as New Jerusalem and hell as a fireplace. In that scenario the need for the leaf of the tree of life to heal the nations seems illogical or needless as there is supposed to be no diseases in the heavenly places; no body dares to give proper elucidation on many of the vision subjects dealt in the book. I too confess that we have not properly understood the mysterious facts regarding an eternal life as described in the Bible. This may be the reason I think common people and even those who are expected to have knowledge are doubtful or feel hard to believe in an eternity after the life in this world. Some people take comfort saying that they do not know of their existence before birth then why bother of that after death.

Let me share my thoughts based on scripture with you.

"Being a means to an end is what gives things a meaning" – Andy Stanley. Being a Christian do we have a designed goal or purpose for our life? Do we lead a life targeting on our goals as per the rules? Are we running our race steadfastly? Do we too think men are created for vanity? (Psalms 89:47……. For what vanity hast thou created all the children of men!). It is high time to ponder over the subject.

> *"The last proceeding of reason is to recognize that there is an infinity of things which are beyond it. There is nothing so conformable to reason as this disavowal of reason".*
>
> *– Blaise Pascal*

Paul says, 'if *in this life only we have hope in Christ we are of all men most miserable.*' 1 Corinthians 15:19. In the story of the rich man and Lazarus the rich man's lifestyle was that he was pleased with the life in this world only. Eat drink and be merry was the philosophy of the man who amassed wealth for him, to whom God said '……*thou fool, this night thy soul shall be required of thee, then who's shall those things be….?*'. Luke 12: 16-21. What God expect from His children is that they shall be "*rich toward God.*" We must get detached from carnal earthly riches and pleasures and be attached towards heavenly riches and pleasures in the presence of God. We are unable to imagine the pleasures in the presence of God and that is the problem with hoping for the unseen. Psalmist says from his experience with God, '*You will make known to me the path of life, in your presence is fullness of joy, in your right hand there are pleasures forever*' Psalm 16:11. When we become rich towards God, only then can we understand our goal and the path to achieve it. Only then can we envision or ideate the rejoicing in the heavenly places. Jesus expressed his wish to his disciples that joy shall be made full in them. John 17:13. How can we even try to understand eternal life unless we know what all things are available there? Bible gives us many clues to understand how it is to be in eternity and how inexpressible the joy prevailing there. We need a mind and spirit to visualize it and experience it in this life too. It is something characteristic, personal, and firm for a believer, not something abstract or vague to pursue. We are asked to seek His kingdom to find it out.

God has made us for an eternal life with Him. The writer of Ecclesiastes got the knowledge, and he writes *"He has made everything beautiful in its time; He has also set eternity in the human heart; yet no one can fathom what God has done from the beginning to end"* Ecclesiastes 3:11(NIV). Some other translation says *".... also he hath set the world in their heart…….".* He says that no human can find the depth of Gods works from eternity to eternity. He is the beginning and the end. God the Father is eternal, the Son is eternal, and the Holy spirit is eternal. Also, eternity is set in the human heart, or the world is set in his heart. Then why we are doubtful about or are unable to discern that eternal life is something definite and it is in us. The world should be in human heart and not his heart in this world. Jesus revealed it in his life. The life of many saints are examples for it. When Stephanus was about to be stoned, he visions the heavenly glory, and it reveals that there is something glorious awaiting us in the hereafter.

Eternity Past

We are born not according to our desire. Our birth time, place, or parents are not chosen by us. It happens! Who is behind it? Who knows. Ecclesiastes: 9:11.When in Ephesians 1:4 Paul states '…… *according as he hath chosen us in Him before the foundation of the world…..'* He affirms the fact that our substance was with God from the beginning of the world. In Psalms 139:15-16 Psalmist says '…… *my substance was not hid from thee, when I was made in secret and curiously wrought in the lowest parts of the earth. Thine* *eyes did **see my substance, yet being unperfect,** and in thy book all my members were written, which in continuance were fashioned, when **as yet there was none of them**.'* In conformity with the words in the Ecclesiastes the psalmist also wonders and exclaims "…. *how precious also are thy thoughts unto me O, God!".* It is a great information even for us which is for our transformation. When in Psalms 90 it is stated, return ye children of men, God is calling us *back* to Him; can't we infer that we were with Him in the past.

Jesus taught his disciples to pray "*thy kingdom come*"; how, when, or where is it to come? Is it not in our hearts when we accept him as our Lord and savior and in this life? (Read Romans 5:1-2 and 8:29-30). In Titus 1:2 *'in hope of eternal life, which God, that cannot lie, promised before the world began…….'.* To whom did He gave the promise before the world began? He is the beginning and the end; He is the God of the present. The promise is for all which we consider in our concept of time dimension as past, present and future.

If things are like this, I think we can come to a point of thought that we too are of eternal existence as manifested through the life of our Lord Jesus Christ. We are allowed or predestinated to live in this world for a short while in a material form to serve some particular purpose of the Almighty God. We have to live according to the will of God in the circumstances and situations where we are put in, with the determination as of Jesus, *'Father ………. not my will, but thine, be done.'* We are in His hands as different tools for His works on this earth which is His creation. We are placed in the proper places and situations in the appropriate periods to serve His purpose. Jesus said, *'My meat is to do the will of Him that sent me and to finish His work'.* Our lives hence become only a part of an eternity which constitutes a past, a present and a future. In this world, as Adam and Eve were placed in Eden, we also are given the freedom to choose between the good and the bad. To choose either eternal life or eternal death. The word of God teaches us clearly what is happening in this world for both good and bad people, both believers and nonbelievers. The truth revealed by the writer of Ecclesiastes is "*…time and chance happen to them all*". Nobody can blame the situations or circumstances they are in. We are created to fit in the right and proper niche: not a random creation. But if we do not serve the purpose of our master, he will chastise us to teach us his will. We have to submit to the chiseling of the Creator without grumbling. If we rebel or disobey, we will be thrown out of the paradise as Adam and Eve. As believers can we be sure that we are moving in the right track and serve the purpose of our Master. How can we know that?

It is a fact that we are ignorant of our past eternity with God. As per Colossians 3 our life is hid with Christ in God. This is about the life of those who are redeemed through Jesus Christ. If so, our past eternity also was hidden in God. About our future eternity we get knowledge from the word of God. Our present is the gap wherein we have to fill with our choice in the light of our knowledge of the Word of God. But many of us believe, eternity is something that is beyond the grave. I heard somebody saying that the life everlasting with Christ can be achieved even at the last moment of leaving the earth. Their role model is the thief on the cross. It is okay, but it is at the dispensation of the Almighty whether one gets the chance to get transformed at the last moment. We have to understand that at the precise time of his knowledge of Jesus, the thief was transformed, he confessed and witnessed his faith in Jesus to his immediate neighbor, that is, he preached gospel. That is what God wants us too to do. From then onwards, when we accept Jesus Christ as our Savior and redeemer and love him in our heart, we will be with him enjoying the life everlasting. In John 14 we see that God loves them who loves Jesus, and the Father and son will live in him. The Holy Spirit also will be in him, and he knows that the Holy Spirit is in him. As those three are everlasting and when the Trinity lives in us, we too become eternal. As in the theory of Osmosis we will be absorbed into eternity. Our image is no more existing, and we will be of the image of Jesus Christ manifesting the glory of God. That is what we call Christianity- to get identified with the identity of Christ. So, our eternal life starts here itself at the very moment we accept Jesus Christ. Paul rightly says in Colossians 1:13 '……. *and has translated us into the kingdom of His son*.' See the tense used here, it is already done regarding the redeemed. Paul again says, '*I have been crucified with Christ and I no longer live, but Christ lives in me* .'Galatians 2:20. Romans 5:7 '…. *count ourselves dead to sin but alive to God in Christ Jesus.* ' Again, in Philpians 1:21 '…*for to me to live is Christ and to die is gain*'. Many more verses we can find in the Word of God assuring us our eternity beginning in this world itself. We become a new creature when we are with Christ. As Paul says we will then rejoice in everything and anything at any time, we are in peace with God and fellow beings through Jesus Christ. We will be peace makers and God's children. That is the seal of the holy spirit and the seal of blood in our forehead. Gentiles will identify us as a separate people and give respect and fear. If we experience eternal life in our Christian life, we will bear the fruits of spirit as stated in Galatians 5:22-24--the inner witness of the holy spirit in conjunction with the outward manifestation of the fruits of the spirit. '*And this is the record, that God has given us eternal life, and this life is in his Son. He that has the Son has life; and he that has not the Son of God has not life. These things have I written unto you that believe on the name of the Son of God; that ye may know that ye have eternal life, and that ye may believe on the name of the Son of God*'. (1 John 5 :11-13). Eternal life is an intimate relationship – ever close—with God our father and Jesus, in this world which even continues in the hereafter. "**The whole range of our Christian life becomes circumscribed by the characteristics of Jesus Christ. Embodying eternal life, Christ becomes a definite object in the consciousness of the believer. Eternal life becomes something characteristic and personal for the believer**". The notion of eternal life is an important subject in interpreting and propagating Christianity.

Why in the present Christian diaspora, Christians are being scorned and contempt in many countries in the society? We can see that the life pattern of most of the so-called believers and exponents of Christianity do not reflect the glory of the Kingdom of God. I think even among Christian preachers, many of them do not believe in eternal life. Otherwise, they would not have behaved in a manner as we see now. Unless we spread the fragrance of the Word, experiencing eternity in our life we cannot influence the society. Our faith will be a farce or flaunt before the public. Our claims of being Christians becomes a deceptive appearance only. Our rhetoric preaching and exhortations become just gimmick and lines drawn on water making no marks or moves in the hearts of the hearers. In the present world, life of leaders is more prone to be evaluated in the public and is more transparent, how hard they try to hide it from the public. Christian leaders should *"walk the talk"* in order to be examples to the herd they shepherd and the world around. Let the so called, titular Christians turn to staunch and committed Christians qualified for the Kingdom of God. It is high time that we turn back to God repent and manifest the personality and individuality of Jesus in all our ways. '*Kingdom of God is ……. Righteousness and peace and joy in the holy spirit*' *(Romans 14:17).* '*….. My heart shall rejoice in your salvation*' *(Psalms13:5).* '*……… believe in Him, you greatly rejoice with joy inexpressible and full of glory*' *(1 Peter 1:8).* This is the experience of eternal life in this world. Many Christians think Christian life as a life in the wilderness comparing it with the life of Israel in the desert. I would like to collate it to the Canaan life of Israel, and Jordan as the experience of salvation. Those who were redeemed through the blood of lamb and wandered in the desert could not reach Canaan because God was not pleased in many of them (1 Corinthians 10:1-5). Also 'But with whom was he grieved forty years? Was it not with them that had sinned, whose carcasses fell in the wilderness?........ for unto us was the gospel preached, as well as unto them (Israel): but the word preached did not profit them, not being mixed with faith in them that heard it' (Hebrews 3:17–4:2). When they reached Canaan, manna stopped, they had to toil to earn their living, they had to break the barriers against them, they have to fight the enemies to possess their God promised inheritance. For we the New Testament people it is the spiritual realm we are in and 'we have to wrestle not against flesh and blood, but against principalities, against powers, against the rulers of the darkness of this world, against spiritual wickedness in high places' (Ephesians 6:12). Also, we are chosen to suffer tribulations for the glorification of Jesus' name, to have fellowship of his sufferings, to be made conformable unto his death and attain unto the resurrection power (Philippians 3:10-11). This is the life of a saved Christian believer. That is the Kingdom life with Jesus Christ. God wants us not to live as fools, but as wise understanding the will of our Lord about each of us (Ephesians 5:15-17). May God allow us to continue the rejoicing, eternally throughout the life here and hereafter wherein we are seated along with Jesus the First born. God bless us.

5

Worship – In Truth and Spirit

During the last two or three decades we have witnessed drastic changes in the world. Though we glorify it as global expansion or growth, the shift seems to have occasioned adverse effects in certain realms of social life to a great extent. We may doubt that peoples have become bereft of moral values in the world around. Globalization has also brought in a market culture of consumerism. When so many countries and peoples have reaped huge material benefits, so many others have fallen prey to this culture and adversely affected in various ways. Stability in family life is facing great threats. The onset of internet and social media have influenced the society enormously, especially youngsters. While we have many areas in the global arena to be proud of, there are quite a few areas where people seem to feel honored in what is shameful. A state similar to what is stated in Romans I:21-32 seems to exist in these days.

Globalization, consumerism, or materialism or by whatever name we call it, it has tightened its c laws on the spiritual world too. Christians have now become "*wise*" enough to outsource even the responsibility of prayers. Youngsters are interested in making worship an entertainment. The present trend is to have loud clamor, singing and yelling in worships, which most often emerge as an emotional outburst inspired by the ambience created by the rhythm of music. The number of churches promoting such worships increased in plenty, recently. We shall be aware that the actions and charades that are not bringing honor to God rather causes dishonor to the name of our Lord.

What does it mean by Worship?

Singing and praising with outstretched hands and bowing and praying are all acts of worship; but they are not everything of worship. They are only a part of the matter. Christian worship is more than that. It is all about the feel and feature of our hearts – the attitude, our focus, our priorities and our lifestyle. Worship is something that spurts from our inner being. It's outcome we see in various situations illustrated in the Bible. What is and what is not worship can be discerned from the Bible teachings. An understanding of he who is worthy to be worshipped is most important when we begin to worship. What is our status before Him, is next to be taken care of.

"The importance of essential Christian doctrine can hardly be overstated. First, these are the very doctrines that form the line of demarcation between the kingdom of Christ and the kingdom of the cults. While we may debate nonessentials without dividing over them, when it comes to essential Christian doctrine there must be unity. Hence, the maxim: In essentials unity, nonessentials liberty, and in all things charity."- Hank Hanegraaff.

God is spirit and they that worship him must worship in spirit and truth (John 4:24). This is the essential doctrine of worshipping God. To comprehend the verses, we must turn to the word of God. Our focus shall be on Jesus Christ and his words. That is why Paul when he writes to Corinthians, he expresses his anxiety that *'their minds may be corrupted from the simplicity that is in Christ'* (NIV). *'Your minds will be led astray from the simplicity and purity of devotion to Christ'* (NASB) 2 Corinthians: 11:3. Most of us are satisfied with our Christian lives. Have we ever paused for a moment to think whether God is satisfied with our lives? Could we make any influence in the society we live in, by our lifestyle, words, or deeds? Do we bear the fruits of the spirit so that people around can enjoy us? If the answer is yes; Then we can confidently say that our worship is a fragrant sacrifice to the Lord. We must individualize and own the word of God for our living on it. *'For unto us the gospel was preached as well as unto them, but the word preached did not profit them, not being mixed with faith in them that heard it'.* (Hebrews 4:2). The word has to be mixed with faith in us personally otherwise it won't profit our Christian life making our worship futile. So, *'Where of be ye not unwise, but understanding what the will of Lord is .... but be filled with the Spirit; speaking to yourselves in psalms and songs, singing and making melody in your heart to the Lord; giving thanks always for all things unto God and the Father in the name of our Lord Jesus Christ; submitting yourselves one to another in the fear of God.' (Ephesians 5:17-21)*

Our worship of God on earth shall be a preparation for the celebrations of praise that will take place in the eternity. (Revelation 22:3). Let us think in the light of the Bible what are the ingredients of true worship, what are various forms of worship, and should there be an order for worship?

> *"Worship has been misunderstood as something that arises from a feeling which 'comes upon you', but it is vital that we understand that it is rooted in a conscious act of the will, to serve and obey the Lord Jesus Christ"*
> *– Graham Kendrick*

There is praise in worship, prayer, fellowship communion, singing, scripture reading, proclamation of the word of God and taking collections in a worship. All on different contexts are seen in the Bible in the Old and New Testaments. We can see examples from the life and experiences of Abraham, Moses, Nehemiah, Daniel, David, Solomon, etc. in the Old Testament and the teachings of Jesus Christ, St. Paul, and other apostles in the New Testament. The prayer Jesus taught his disciples gives us the perfect model of prayer as well as worship. All the ingredients of worship can be seen there. Most of the Psalms are songs, praises, prayers, and meditations.

It is a great experience to have space for worship by individuals in church worships providing opportunities to sing, testify and glorify God along with other members joining in their rejoicing and praising. This kind of open worship is practiced in many churches together with liturgical worship or exclusively.

God called us to the praise of His glory. (Ephesians 1:4-12, Isaiah 43:7, Jeremiah 13:11)

Praise is the joyful thanksgiving adoration or glorification of the Almighty God – the celebration of His goodness, kindness, provision, and grace. The act of praising is rightfully due to Him (Psalms 24, 95.96.). Psalm 150 illustrates the when, why, and how of praising the Lord. By praising God our awareness of the greatness of God is revived and renewed every time. It makes us enjoy the grace and the presence of God throughout our lives. (Psalm 135:3). It is the most pleasant experience for a believer. The praise and worship of the weaklings causes God to move on their behalf to ordain them with strength (Psalm 8:2). The collective praising and singing of the goodness, greatness and mercy of the Lord in one mind and in one sound transforms the spiritual environment. (2 Chronicles 5:13-14). Further, we see in Psalm 22:3 that God inhabits the atmosphere of praise. If we want to see the clear manifestation of God's blessings all we need to do is to praise him with our heart, mind, and soul. Paul exhorts the church of Corinth to glorify God in their body and spirit which are of God's. (1 Corinthians 6:19-20). Our praise shall be of uniform spirit and mind when we join to worship collectively as each one is a member of the body of Christ. Worshipping God in fellowship with other believers is a great blessing. In the book of Acts, we see the disciples and other believers of *one accord* gathering as Jesus told them and receiving the Holy Spirit. The effect of being of one mind is seen in Acts 4:32-35 .

Lord's Supper is another form of worship. (Acts 20:7, 1 Corinthians 10:14-17, 11:25-27).

We cannot ignore the importance of Lord's supper in our worship. It is the seat of our deepest thoughts and emotions concerning our faith, only for which we are qualified to worship God. It is a time of repentance by which we access the sanctum sanctorum of the tabernacle. Holy communion as enjoyed by the apostles; we can say is a part of true worship. 'And they continuing daily with *one accord* in the temple, and breaking bread from house to house, did eat their meat with *gladness and singleness of heart*, praising God and having favor with all the people' (Acts 2:46-47)

Prayer – the humble form of worship

Prayer is the next form of worship. It is the instrument of our communication with the Lord. In prayer we get the feel of the spiritual link with our heavenly father. It is the most modest form, I think, in our worship. But our usual prayers have become just submission of our petitions. We need not have any place or time to get

> *True prayer is a way of life, not just for use in cases of emergency. Make it a habit, and when the need arises you will be in practice*
> *– Billy Graham*

connected with God. Only thing is that we keep ourselves always within His reach. His ears are always open for our prayers. Enoch experienced that presence always in his life. We also shall present our bodies a living sacrifice, holy, acceptable unto God which is our reasonable service (Romans 12:1). God wants us, as a father, to submit our needs before him with praises - and of course according to His will about us. To know His will about us we have to be always in communication with Him. For that we must be holy as He is. Our Lord wants us to come to his foot stool with a heart of repentance and forgiveness and complete surrender of our whole mind and body. Our prayers to be accepted in heaven in the golden vials (Revelations 5:8) we shall come before God, pure in heart. Our worship in prayers shall be like the prayer of David - 'Accept my prayer as incense offered to you, and my upraised hands as an evening offering' (Psalms 141:2 NLT).

Study of Scripture is vital in Worship

Scripture reading and proclamation of the word of God directs us for meditation and to have an introspection on us. It is highly important to have a detailed understanding of the word of God because our prayers are answered through the word and God's will about us is manifested through the word. The word enables us to understand, the things which God has prepared for those who love Him (1 Cor 2:9), learn God's riches, Christ's fullness, and the divine bounties. God reveals all of them to us through the scriptures. His word …" ïs a lamp unto my feet and a light unto my path". (Psaslm119:105). Psalm119 is much inspirational for a believer. It manifests the glory of the word of God. The word is the daily bread that we pray for, every day. We get divine wisdom only through the Scripture." *I have more understanding than all my teachers: for thy testimonies are my meditation. I understand more than the ancients because I keep thy precepts."* (Ps 119:99-100)). Word is the way to eternal life (John 1:1, 14). Many times, we fail to understand the word in its true meaning so that we err in many things. We often fail to discern things which are told in the Bible in its spiritual meaning rather we take it verbatim. Jesus himself pointed it out to the disciples (E.g.: John 4:32-34, 6:56-63). What is worship we must understand from various biblical contexts, and experiences of godly people mentioned in the Bible.

How collection of offertory becomes a part of worship?

Taking collection is also a part of worship in our church meetings. Paul says". ..God loves the cheerful giver". The liberality of the church of Macedonia is an example for all the Christians. "The administration of this service not only supplies the want of saints, but is abundant also by many thanksgiving unto God". (2 Corinthians 9:13, Romans 15:26-27). Thanksgiving is an important ingredient in worship so arousing many thanks to God is also a part of worship, I would like to say.

Conclusion

"Christian worship involves praising God in music and speech, readings from scripture, prayers of various sorts, a sermon and various holy ceremonies (often called sacraments) such as the Eucharist". "Worship is reverent honor and homage paid to God".

Whatever be the form we select to praise and worship our Lord it shall be in truth and spirit. The holy and mighty name of God shall be glorified. We shall be confident that God is pleased in our praise. It is good to have an order in worship in churches. Paul reminds that "*Let everything be done decently and in order.*" Combining all components of worship our forefathers have compiled an order for the liturgical worship in the churches. If we follow the order in one mind and spirit worship will be a blessing. Paul appreciates the church of Colossi for their order and steadfastness. Also, he directed the Corinthian church that everything shall be decent and in order. It is better to have a written order for the collective regular worship, to maintain decency and order in worship. Contextually, we may opt for worships in partial forms. What is important is that we be living sacrifices pleasing to God.

Nevertheless, we are compelled during the periods of the spreading of Covid-19 all over the world that we should rethink our worship forms. Henceforth, we have been worshipping according to our satisfaction and our interpretation of the word. God wants everyone individually to examine whether we are in true faith and our worship is in Holy Spirit. Through prophet Isaiah God tells the house of Judah during the periods of Uzziah, Jotham, Ahaz and Hezekiah a period before the exile of Judah about their rebellion against God their father. God rebukes and reprimands them about their worships (Isiah 1: 10-15). God says, I am weary of bearing them. Then God tells them how to worship Him after cleansing themselves of all their blemishes. It is high time for all believers to settle the matter with God. God has revealed us of all unnecessary rituals which were hitherto considered as *sine-qua-non* in our worships. So, our mode of worship in collective form shall become a unity of believers who cleanse themselves of all blemishes and submit themselves as a living sacrifice pleasing to God to form a part of the body of Jesus Christ, the church. To build the church on the foundation of our Lord Jesus Christ the stones shall agree with the foundation. Each one shall be reconciled with God through Jesus. The temple of Jerusalem was demolished as Jesus predicted, in AD 70, thereby annihilating the temple concept of the Jews. We know how Jesus described the temple of Jerusalem (Matthew 21:13). Jesus also said, *"my temple will be called a house of prayer"*. Every believer is a temple of prayer wherein God lives. During the period of the spread of Corona virus, I think, believers could have understood the meaning of true worship and prayer both individually and collectively.

Jesus through his cross has opened the way for all who believe to enter unto the mercy seat of the Almighty; doing away with the priestly supremacy, we too are called to a royal priesthood. We, all the believers, are called to take up the responsibility and rights incumbent in our new status and position endowed on us, through Jesus Christ in our spiritual lives. Obeying the word of God whole heartedly and submissively is true worship of God. Some of the churches still follow the hierarchy of the priesthood of Aron. They are doing it not because of ignorance of the word of God but to keep their followers in a fearful ambience all the time to run the church as a profitable establishment. They won't enter the kingdom and will not allow others also enter the kingdom of God. Paul has suggested services of different members of the church according to the grace given to them from above for the benefit of the fellowship of believers and for their spiritual edification. True worship or adoration is due only to God. *"It is the manifestation of submission, and acknowledgement of dependence, appropriately shown towards the excellence of an uncreated divine person and to his absolute Lordship"*- St. Thomas Aquinas. But, as time passed by, this system for worship with various assignments in services turned out to be the offices of authority as was in the case of Jewish priesthood. About such shepherds, through prophet Ezekiel God tells, "Woe be to the shepherds of Israel that do feed themselves! Should not the shepherds feed the flocks?" As we have only one shepherd who has given his life for the flocks, all the believers are the flocks of that good shepherd Jesus Christ. Our worship will become pleasing to God when we are all in peace and like- minded with God through Jesus Christ. No more there shall be sheep and shepherd in this world only church the bride, and bridegroom, our Lord. Those who honor and glorify God by worshipping in truth and spirit will find themselves in the bride's costume when our Lord descends in midair to receive her. True and wise worshippers will get entrance with the bridegroom to the marriage. *"Her wedding dress is dazzling, lined with gold by the weavers; all her dresses and robes are woven with gold. She is led to the king.........a grand entrance to the king's palace!"*. God bless us.

6

Be Self-Aware,
Be Not Self-Righteous

The society we live in is comprised of people of different faith, culture, social background, ideologies etc. Each person differs from the other in intelligence, feelings, emotions, and behavioral patterns. To be in peace with people of differing nature and keeping the society united is achieved through give- in and give-out policies and maintaining certain moral standards, self-imposed or statutorily imposed. It is quite natural that conflicts arise occasionally among persons, groups, sects, religions, and countries. Globalization has made the world more condensed, and peoples have become more closely connected. In certain areas of interactions compromise is practiced and in certain other areas conflicts seems widened. The situation of spreading of viruses worldwide is an extant demerit of globalization, I think. The scripture provides us with the guidelines how to deal with in any situations.

A secular study of the nature and behavioral pattern of man can be made based on the theory of human needs formulated by Abraham Maslow.

Figure: Abraham Maslow's theory of human needs

In this theory the base of the pyramid is physiological needs i.e., food and shelter and the pinnacle of the pyramid is self-actualization. Self-actualization is the point where the mortal man meets with the Divine.

The paradox we see at present universally is that people do not go beyond the second stage. The area of food, shelter and safety gets wider and wider for most of the people. None are satisfied ever in their basic needs. Love and belongingness in most of the cases seems pretention. Esteem, most of the people think, is based on their worldly possessions of wealth and positions which serve their basic needs only. We can also see some fake coins supposing themselves to be holy claim to have reached the self -actualization stage in the present society. It seems mysterious for the mortals to reach the fifth stage in Maslow's theory by satisfying the human needs.

A soul-searching is necessary time and again for all people especially those who are called by the name of Christ. A thoughtfulness of the state of faith is a must. Christian believers are not called to be just like the heathen. There is a benchmark fixed for us as Christians which is nothing less than being holy where our hope and goal meets with the will of God. In the common parlance people use the words self-awareness, self-realization, self-righteousness, as synonyms without differentiating. Let us discuss the difference between self-righteousness and self-awareness in the light of scripture and some secular definitions.

Often people are heard making statements such as "I have said /done it according to my conviction". We too might have come to such occasions of making the same statement. We say it to prove that we are righteous. It may be due to our cognitive bias that we hold on to our stand of being righteous. *But Christian faith wants us to view the situation from the angle of Gods righteousness.*

Self-righteousness is "*Exhibiting smug or unwarranted confidence in one's own righteousness*". Self-righteous people cannot often tolerate the opinions and behavior of others. They exhibit an attitude that they are morally superior to the average people and are of greater virtue than others.

We can equip ourselves with the right-living qualities by analyzing certain attributes of self- righteous people that is revealed in their behavior and manner as per secular studies which is contrary to God's righteousness revealed through the Bible.

1. **Whiter than white**. They feel and assert that their part is always right, and they claim to be self-aware (without knowing the depth of the phrase). They are faultless and without error as per social expectations and moral principles, they are impeccable they assume.

2. **I am my own**. They keep themselves away from others assuming for themselves a special status - "Someone in particular" in the society. An attitude that "I am my own". A type of stoic people.

3. **Elitism**. They feel superior in intelligence, knowledge, wealth, and social standing and demand special positions in the society/ groups.

4. **Vanity**. Excessive pride in their appearance and / or accomplishments: smug or show off people.

5. **Holier-than -thou.** They pretend to be holier than others in the group or society. We see such people very often in churches. They can be identified by their deeds which they do clandestinely.

Self- righteous are self-centered, self-complacent, self-motivated, and heavily trying to create an image for themselves. They claim that they are self-aware.

"Humans are fairly accurate in their perceptions of others, but generally inaccurate in their perceptions of themselves. Humans tend to judge others by their behavior, but they think they have special information about themselves – that they know what they are really like inside – and thus effortlessly find ways to explain away selfish acts and maintain the illusion that they are better than others "- Robert Wright.

In this present world we are prone to evaluate such persons as admirable and having good personality and integrity. We tend to qualify them with adjectives such as self-made, self-motivated and so. In the Bible we can see such people among pharisees, scribes and priests. Jesus says to the disciples and his followers '…except your righteousness shall exceed the righteousness of the scribes and pharisees, ye shall in no case enter into the kingdom of heaven'. Matthew 5:20. They are the people appointed or rather supposedly anointed to teach the righteousness of the Almighty God. But they could not reach up to the norms expected of them. It is said about them that they observed the law given through Moses. It is also said about them that they observed the law in hypocrisy. Everything they did was done for men to see. Jesus called them "whitewashed tombs". They are exhorted to "cleanse the inside of the cup and platter". (Matthew 23). Here we see the difference. Biblical righteousness is the up-righteousness and right standing with God. It does not come through living a holy life rather holiness comes from being righteous, and the fulfillment of laws come from being righteous. It may seem incongruent, but it is simple and comprehensible with God as we receive the gift of God's righteousness through Jesus Christ (Romans 5:1).

We must have a thorough understanding of *righteousness apart from God* and *righteousness with God.*

We are familiar with the story of the wedding banquet in Matthew 22:1-14 . Here when the invitees did not attend the King's banquet the King extended the invitation to all in the street. All those attended were gifted wedding clothes. It is customary to wear clothes suitable for a a wedding banquet. We see one person present who did not have suiatbel wedding attire . Why didn't he wear what was given to all who were entitled to attend the party ? Was he not given the clothes? No! He was offered the gift, but he rejected to wear it and believed that his own clothes were appropriate to attend the feast. We know what happened to him. This person represents the self-righteous people, and the others represent those who accept the gift of God's righteousness. God's righteousness is the clothing given to his faithful through Jesus Christ. He makes our righteousness "shine like the dawn".

In Matthew 6:1-2 we see Jesus saying 'Be careful not to practice your righteousness in front of others to be seen by them. If you do, you will have no reward from your father in heaven'. '…. Truly I tell you, they have received their reward in full'. Self-righteousness has an end in itself.

The prayer of the pharisee and the tax collector in Luke 18: 9-14 is another example. The pharisee's prayer shows that he is dominated or obsessed by his virtue, and he compares himself with the tax collector who according to him is a sinner. We can see all the attributes of a self-righteous person engrossed in his personality. Whereas we see the tax collector as a person who longs for God's righteousness to work in him. Gods' righteousness when revealed in us leads us towards self-awareness.

Self-awareness

When we are blessed with the righteousness of God, as we accept salvation through the atoning sacrifice of Jesus Christ, the holy spirit starts working in us teaching us and reminding us of what Jesus taught about sin, righteousness, and judgement. The understanding of these themes provides us with the basics of self-awareness which is objective in nature, a realization of our inner and outer self with all its limitations and potentials, sins, and virtues. *Unlike self-righteousness as per human perceptions which ends, self-awareness is objective leading towards a goal.* As Christians our goal is getting reconciled with God through Jesus Christ. So, self-awareness as a Christian is concerned is an evaluation of our spiritual and moral state in relation to the standard that God set for us. If we succeed in the process of identifying and defining the gap between the two components namely the standard that God fix for us and the state we are at present in, it will push us ahead to reach the God fixed level. This process we can name as self-awareness, and it leads us to self-actualization.

Self-awareness is defined by psychologists and philosophers in different ways.

"It is an awareness of one's own individuality and personality"-a common thinking. It is not self-consciousness, which is an awareness of one's environment, body and lifestyle. It is, how an individual consciously knows and understands his own character, feelings, motives, and desires. It should be a progressive affair in one's life.

"When we focus our attention on ourselves, we evaluate and compare our internal standards and virtues, we become self-conscious as objective evaluators of ourselves"- It is a mechanism of self-control. – *Shelly Dual and Robert Wicklund* (Theory of self-awareness)

It is *"Knowing one's internal states, preferences, resources and intuitions"*. *"It is the keystone to emotional intelligence"* - Daniel Goleman.

The ability to monitor our emotions and thoughts from moment to moment is key to understanding ourselves better. Self-awareness makes us to be in peace within and proactively manage our feelings, emotions, and behavior. Self-awareness gives us a positive outlook in life and makes us more compassionate. It benefits for an individual's personality development and improvement in social relations. Self-awareness is knowing our potential and inner resources, rather than knowing what we are.

It is an all-encompassing awareness we have of ourselves in the past, in the present and of our expectation for the future. This enables us to envision an ideal self for ourselves. In the present universal society people often use the phrase self-awareness to masquerade their self righteous attitude or rather their self-ignorance. Objective self-awareness leads us to self-esteem which is an approval or acceptance we receive from the people or group around us. Mere show-off or big talk will not attract sincere appreciation from others.

Self-esteem is a superior need of the fourth stage in the basic human need's theory of Abraham Maslow.

Self-actualization is the aim in life for most of the religions. But all of them miss the path to reach there. We know Jesus is the only way, the truth and life. "Know thyself" is a great aphorism inscribed in the vestibule of the temple of Apollo in Delphi, Greece. Socrates comments on it "But I have no leisure for them at all; and the reason .... is this; I am not yet able as the Delphic inscription has it, to know myself…." He says it seems ridiculous for him to think over it. Similar inscription of a Sanskrit verse is seen at Sabarimala temple in Kerala, S.India also- "Tat twam asi" meaning *it is you.* As Socrates said, who so ever seeks to understand its meaning will fail unless the right path is chosen. "Knowing one-self" was the philosophy propagated through centuries back as the first step to know God. But as Socrates most people miserably fail in understanding even at the first step to know God. Some people isolate themselves from material pleasures and limit all the basic needs to the barest minimum to reach self-actualization. I think many of them are proving to be fake.

We may look into an incident in Jesus' life on earth. Jesus through his various discourses and his deeds proved to his disciples and followers that he is the son of God. Even then he wants them to testify to that. Jesus wants them to convince themselves and declare that his life, words, and deeds correlate each other, and he is truly the son of God. He asks them who do you think I am? Jesus among other things wants his disciples to understand what is actualization and esteem that a man of God should achieve in this world. *Jesus, as the son of man, projects himself as a role model for all the believers.* Esteem is the acceptance received from others on their evaluation of one's words and deeds. The disciples could know and enjoy the bliss of that state after the resurrection. Paul experienced it. His awareness elevated him to a summit of realization that *"I have been crucified with Christ; and I no longer live but Christ lives in me".* And "But what things were gain to me, those I counted loss for Christ. Yea doubtless, and I count all things but loss for the excellency of the knowledge of Christ Jesus my Lord; for whom I have suffered the loss of all things, and do count them but dung, that I may win Christ".

In biblical terms we can explain self- actualization seen in Human need's theory through the words of Jesus in John 14:20 "At that day ye shall know that I am in my father, and ye in me, and I in you".

This state can be attained when we are going up each step having an awareness and eagerness to reach the summit of the pyramid. But we who are of Christian faith can easily reach the pinnacle observing the guidelines given by Jesus and following him. There is sufficient reason for us to praise our God and glorify Him as our way is open through the cross of Jesus Christ. Whoever opts for this way can reach the pinnacle of self-actualization.

'Examine yourselves, whether ye be in the faith; prove your own selves. Know ye not your own selves, how that Jesus Christ is in you, except ye be reprobates'. 2 Corinthians 13:5. St Paul exhorts the Corinthian church to examine themselves whether they are in faith. The same call is for all the believers in Christ. Examining ourselves is for bridging the gap in our faith level. The disciples ask Jesus at one time to increase their faith. The need of examining ourselves is to increase our faith day by day to a level of confidence as Paul puts it "I have fought a good fight, I have finished my course, I have kept the faith". Self-awareness will ennoble us to a glorious level through our faith in Jesus.

We have to understand what is there and what will be like in the stage of self-actualization. It will promote us to a level where we consider ourselves beyond the limitations of all earthly dimensions! It is very clear in the scriptures. In the mission of attaining self-actualization through self-awareness- for Christian believers ***winning Christ***- we have to forsake all those pleasures luring us in the lower levels of our basic needs, as dung. It is pathetic to see that many Christians along with heathens are running behind this dung. Our seeking of carnal pleasures creates a siege in our way towards the eternal God and His Kingdom.

Regarding the scribes and pharisees he says they say the laws but do it not. This is what we see in the present world even among Christians. St. Paul and many saints attained that glorious state of self-actualization. About them it is said that "of whom the world was not worthy". Even now we can see many people who keeps themselves in the backstage saying to the Lord I am your servant I have done only what I am obliged to do. They do not want a trumpet to be sounded or a drum beaten when they do something for the glory of God. They do not value much of their lives even. Their hope is not in this world. They are least concerned about "what shall we eat? What shall we drink? Or wherewithal shall we be clothed?". We may praise the Lord for them and follow their example.

'For, God hath not appointed us for wrath; but to attain salvation by our Lord Jesus Christ'. "For, this is the will of God, even our sanctification. That ye should abstain from fornication". "For God hath not called us unto uncleanness, but unto holiness". God wants us "to come unto the knowledge of truth"- foreseeing the eternal life in the presence of God where there is happiness and rejoicing.

It is necessary that in this world we need to satisfy our basic needs to live healthy, comfortable, and godly lives to reach the highest point of becoming holy as God is holy. But in each stage God wants us to be content at a certain level. The rich man who came to Jesus seeking how could he attain actualization or eternal life returned sad and heavy hearted because he could not assimilate the idea of relinquishing his worldly possessions. Paul when giving directions to Timothy to teach the church says believers are to be content with if they are "having food and raiment" (1 Timothy 6:8-10). I think the idea conveyed is "the bare-minimum". We should be aware of our saturation level about all our possessions in the light of Jesus' teachings. "Lay up for yourselves treasures in heaven" – that is what God expect from us. A study of one's beingness based on Christian spirituality rather than an ontological study only can make one successful in life. Such an awareness of our "being" motivates us towards actualization.

What is our conception about ourselves? Are we self-righteous or self-aware? Paul tells the Ephesians, "Be very careful, then, how you live-not as unwise but as wise". Contemporary English Version puts it like "Act like people with good sense and not like fools". Yes, it is for all Christians. Let us think over it and be sensible in our life. May God help us.

7

Marriage – To Have and to Hold

Whosoever findeth a wife findeth a good thing, and obtaineth favor of the Lord' (Proverbs 18:22). The basic thought that gives us confidence is that God's favor is there, upon a Christian family to live triumphantly. Of late we are seeing drastic changes in attitudes and approaches among the youngsters about marriage, choosing their life partners based on certain conceptions which they think right, and elders think wrong, particularly among Christian families. Role of parents in marriage of their children is minimized to the role of planning for the marriage if at all necessary. I am not attempting to judge or establish which system is good or which is bad. All communities are prone to this change and the Christian community is not an exception. Even though we claim to be a separate people having a divine code of conduct for the day today life, our life pattern does not seem to comply with such disciplines in many spheres of life. Our life also seems to be like the rest of the people whom we call gentiles. The old concept in marriage was that the *summum bonum* of the girls' life is to please her husband and the in-laws, in some traditional eastern cultures. The role of the husband is of a dominant patriarch and that of wife is an obedient help mate. The older pattern of "husband domination and wifely submission" was perhaps easy to achieve. The present pattern of partnership and companionship in marriage is much more difficult to pull on smoothly for a lifetime. This may be the reason for the unprecedented upsurge in divorces and troubled marriages. Bible says, "And the Lord God took the man and put him into the garden of Eden to dress it and to keep it" and "God made Eve as a help meet for Adam." (Genesis 2:15-18). Both are given assignments involving duties and responsibilities in a wide spectrum. Marriage and Family is a subject of great importance now to debate as it constitutes the very foundation of the universal society. At least in the Christian diaspora we must talk about it seriously.

An ideal marriage requires many mature adjustments, understanding, submission and love. The saddest thing in most marriages is that the partners just become roommates, meal-mates, and bedmates and remain strangers. They may have everything including children born to them. They also have frustrations, neurosis, and perhaps affairs – and live on the edge of boredom and despair. Instead of communicating their feelings, their self, their dreams they speak about casual silly things which according to Paul are a waste.

People around us from other communities' value marriage life as a sacred affair and lead healthier and happy family life. Then what difference does it make for a Christian family? Do the people around us find anything different in our family life? Or could we make any influence as a Christian family in the society we live in? Unlike any other religions our religion is named Christianity and not Christianism. It is not an ..ism like Hinduism, Jainism, Buddhism, Islamism etc. or like socialism, communism or terrorism following a lifestyle based on certain ideology or dogmas. Christianity is forming an identity with Christ our savior who is the way the truth and life. It is not only a lifestyle but life itself. "Therefore, if any man be in Christ, he is a new creature." (2 Corinthians 5: 17). So, we are a different people sanctified to reflect the image of Jesus Christ in our personal, family, and societal life. It is true that the whole humankind is created by God, but all are not children of

God. John 1:12 tells that those who receive Jesus Christ can only become the children of God. But He provides for the needs of all His creations. He showers His blessings (may be material blessings only) on all men good and bad. Psalms 147:9 says "He giveth to the beast his food and to young ravens which cry". Then what makes us different is that we are predestinated unto the adoption of children according to the good pleasure of his will **to the praise of the glory of his grace** (Ephesians 1:5,6).

Marriage - Holy

Let us turn to the Bible to see what it says about married life. It is true that we all know what Bible says but could we absorb the essence and taste the sweetness and spread the aroma of a biblical Christian family. Based on the previous paragraph, through our family life we have to praise the glory of his grace. That is the standard or benchmark for every Christian in every walk of life and especially the standard expected in our family life. From the very first chapter in the Bible, through out, we can feel how much our creator is concerned with marriage and family life of his people.

Gen 1:27 says, 'So God created man in his own image, in the image of God created he him, male and female he created them'. V 26 'let us make man in our own image after our likeness ….'. In these verses we see the plurality of God and at the same time God is singular. This we may say is the concept of Trinity revealed by God at the very beginning of the Bible. This is the likeness of God in which he created man also. Man is a trinity of body, soul, and spirit. The trinity of God can well be explained through the trinity of man. There is nothing mysterious or inexplainable about trinity of God if we understand correctly what man is. Again, man is made male and female, and hence the trinity of man gets perfection when man and woman become one flesh. Man exclaims on seeing the woman "……this is now bone of my bones and flesh of my flesh …. **she was taken out of man**…. Therefore, shall a man …cleave unto his wife and they shall be one flesh". (Genesis 2:23-24). It makes me imagine that the first man created by God was a single unit of man and woman and the feminine part was removed afterwards when God found that it was not good for man to be "alone" which I may translate as "single". So, the concept of marriage is that of a reunion of the separated personality into a single entity "one flesh" and to accomplish the purpose of God and enter the union with God. Since it is all God's own work it is holy. *"Bible teach us that God created marriage to make husbands and wives* **holy** *not just to make them happy"*. -June Hunt.

How to Bond Together

It is the talents that God gave man and woman that makes them fit into each other's lives, just as in a jigsaw puzzle, to form a perfect entity suitable for the kingdom of God. Jesus Christ as the head and church as the body forming a single unit is the ideal image of marriage as seen in the Bible. Being born and brought up in different circumstances and environments totally alien to each other, there will be areas where both the partners will feel it difficult to adjust suitably. Here is the place where we must exercise our God given talents and grace to grind or cut some protruding areas willingly and happily to fit the pieces together and tesselate the surface smooth and joint free. The partners in marriage must cultivate this attitude in order to make the married life enjoyable and pleasing to others. Paul in his epistle to Philippians, despite the hardships caused to him by others, says "…and I there in do rejoice, yea, and will rejoice". (Philippians 1:18"). So, it is our choice to rejoice. It is our attitude that makes the difference. If each partner purposefully decides to have a happy married life, let he/she decide to please, complement and make happy the spouse in the family life rather than seeking own pleasure and comfort. Happiness must be earned. In marriage it is a matter of mutual co-operation with patience, mutual consideration, and acceptance to make the life enjoyable. It is to be accepted that we cannot change certain things which are out of our control. One has to pray, "God give me the *sense* to accept such realities. Give me the *courage* to change things that I can and the *wisdom* to know the difference". True companionship grows within the marriage relationship when there is emotional, spiritual, and physical unity and intimacy (Song of Songs 2:16). Realize that God has not created any person to meet all your needs perfectly. It is the duty of the couples to make each other perfect and that is life and that is the purpose of marriage. Problems arise so that one can spot out one's imperfections. Be confident in the truth that one's identity is in Christ and not in his/her mate.

Bible the User guide

Bible says man is created male and female. It implies that both are not of the same nature or equal in any respect. Only thing is that both are created by God as humankind entirely different from other creations. They are physically different in appearance and structure, emotionally different, feels differently, thoughts, attitudes, temper etc. etc. are all different. In marriage we must learn to mix and match all these by ourselves to make a perfect combination useful for the purpose of God. That is the great task God assigns us through marriage. The Bible is so intriguing, inspiring and engaging for acquiring the skill needed for a meaningful and healthy family life. If we can use any gadgets with the help of a user manual coming along with it, is it not easy for us to follow the directions, very specific and accurate, for making our marriage life enjoyable.

When somebody decides to marry and finds his/her spouse, from then onwards God's favor he/she is getting. His eyes always watch us from His quiet place. When we turn left or right, He will whisper in gentle voice which way we have to walk. Proper understanding of the Bible will help us lead a happy family life.

To Have and to Hold

The headship of husband is to be acknowledged and accepted in Christian families to exhibit the concept of church and Jesus Christ through the family life. Husband is to love his wife as she is taken out of his body and so she is a part of his own person. He must honor and love his wife considering her weakness. Couples together become heirs for grace (Ephesians 5:21-33, Colossians 3:18-21,1 Corinthians11:3,1 Peter 3:7). Both husband and wife shall be submissive to the divine purpose of God. When each one determines to submit it becomes the submission to the interests of the other one within their God given authority. Marriage is a relationship *to have and to hold* till the end of life. God's purpose for marriage is to model Christ and his relationship with the church, a beautiful portrait of sacrificial love. Marriage is designed to reflect the intimate relationship between Christ and his church. Many people think that submission is obedience, but it is not. *Submission is voluntarily yielding to the will of another, whereas obedience is to comply with the commands of another. Submission is an inner attitude of the heart, whereas obedience is the outer act of conformity. Submission never requires violating God's words. It never makes you to violate your conscience as your conscience is God given and a spiritual aspect. It does not require an act that does not glorify God.* Husbands need to address even the minor concerns of their wives and wives in turn should be in tune to their husbands' concern. Thoughtfully serving one another reflects the heart of Christ.

Parties in marriage

Marriage is a relationship which binds two individuals legally together and it is for a lifetime. It is true for all people Christian or gentile. (Corinthians 7:39, Romans 7:1-3). Marriage is said to be a covenant made between two persons who are eligible to contract to live together as husband and wife. When it is legally recorded the persons agree that they will be guided by the law of the land regarding marriage. Christian marriage is also governed by the law of the land. But we, above all other things, attribute a divine perspective for marriage. We consider it as a covenant made by two individuals **with** God rather than in the presence of God. God is not a witness for marriage, but He is a party to the covenant, in my opinion. I think that is why Paul exhorts the Ephesians to submit themselves to one another *in the fear of God* (Ephesians 5:21). The marriage vow even though it seems to be administered to each one, the couples recite the vow as an undertaking before God which shall not be revoked unilaterally. (Matthew 19:6)

Un-realistic expectations

"I pity the couple who expects too much from one another. It is a foolish woman who expects her husband to be to her that which only Jesus Christ can be; ready to forgive, totally understanding, tender and loving, unfailing in every area, anticipating every need, and making more than adequate provision. Such expectations put a man under an impossible strain. And the same goes for the man who expects too much from his wife". – Ruth Bell Graham. Unrealistic expectations sabotage more marriages than anything else. Look beyond the flaws or shortcomings of your mate and try to see his/her needs.

> *"A perfect marriage is just two imperfect people who refuse to give up on each other"*
>
> *– quote*

Ask yourself this question, "what are the deepest root issues that are motivating my spouse to treat me this way? Is there anything I can do Lord to minister to those needs?" If I am guilty woe to me (Job10:15). Hope deferred makes the heart sick (Proverbs 13:12). When joined in wedlock the first preference of the spouse is the loyalty to the partner. Man *leaves* his father and mother. The woman *forgets* her people and her father's house. (Genesis 2:24-25, Psalms 45:10). They are then *bonded* together and become one. They become *transparent* to each other (Genesis 2:25). This translation should take place after marriage in the couples' life. Every man shall have his own wife and every woman her own husband. Any relationship outside the marriage relationship amounts to fornication. (1 Corinthians 7:1-2 Hebrews 13:4). Those couples will truly be happy who acquire sufficient wisdom not to expect the impossible from their marriage, from themselves or from each other.

Purpose of Marriage

The purpose of marriage as God envisages is that there shall be a partnership between each other as we see in Song of Songs 2:16 "my beloved is mine and I am his…..". God expects good parenting from couples. And live enjoying each other. *Partnership, parenting, and pleasure* are God's purpose in marriage for the couples. "I belong to my beloved and his desire is for me" shall be the attitude and approach of each spouse. (Song of Songs 7:10) **Divorce is never an option for differences in marriage**. God hates it (Malachi 2:16). Also, it makes a devastating effect on a wide circle of relationships and especially on children if they have. Children will experience an overwhelming fear, anxiety, and a sense of insecurity. Regardless of the circumstances that follows the marriage the couples have to honor the commitment they made *to God*. God reveals his relationship with his people through Hosea in chapter 2 verses 19 & 20.

The three God given inner needs of human being to be satisfied through marriage are **1)** *Need for love* **2)** *Significance* **and 3)** *Security*. From creation, by nature, man's need for significance is greater, whereas woman's need for security is bigger and deeper. And need for love is supreme in both and the other needs are satisfied when the feel of belongingness and love blooms in the marriage. Both husband and wife should become aware of the partner's needs and learn to meet them creatively.

Troubled Marriages

We may be familiar with many families and their lives . It is true that so many troubled families are around us. But all of them pull on. There are various kinds of problems in families but without finding a solution they try to adjust with momentary seize fire solutions. When one party may keep silent for some time, one may make a walk out and stay somewhere for a while. Some may take refuge in drink or in the company of friends. This will occur continually, and the basic problems remain unaddressed till the end. Such hell like atmosphere prevails in many Christian families even though solution is easily available with us. Many people dare to say that even if God the Lord tries, this man/woman won't get right. In the present conditions nobody from outside, even if near relations, won't get involved. These are *make-believe marriages*. Both are stubborn in nature, always defensive, rejecting mate's feelings, selfish, not displaying affection – apathetic, manipulative etc. Is a Christian not aware of the biblical family concept?

Another type of troubled marriage is *Maladjusted Marriage*. In such type of marriage, the couples do not experience the emotional expression of physical oneness. As an act of love God's design is that both partners yield their bodies to one another. If physical intimacy is not there in a family, it may affect even the mental equilibrium of partners.

The third type is *Mixed-up marriage,* having conflicting values over religious belief, parenting responsibilities, marital commitments, social connections, friendship choices, moral principles etc. Such marriages create power struggle, tension, and criticism. God's design is that they be like minded, having the same desires and purposes. Many inter-religious marriages and marriages between persons of different social status are prone to such problems.

Another area where trouble pops up is that of finance. Such *Money-troubled marriages* experience disagreement over how income should be earned and spent, how budget be prepared and followed, fixing priorities, how difference in budget or lack of money shall be dealt with etc. God desires that a marriage shall be free of emphasis on money.

> *" A good marriage is the union of two good forgivers. "*
> *– Ruth Bell Graham*

When in marriage the couples fail to recognize and respond to the God given duties and responsibilities it becomes a *Misaligned Marriage* in Christian perspective. Failures are mainly in the following aspects. Spiritual involvement and leadership, financial responsibility, decision making, responsibility in finding solutions, *proper* communication, responsibility to express emotional attachment, etc. It is not fair for a spouse to make bitter or sarcastic statements or to be stubborn on matters. God's plan for man is to feel a sense of significance through both providing for his family and receiving the love and respect of wife; Also, he is used by God to be a source of security for his wife through his love, acceptance, and sensitivity to her desires.

Conclusion

When Solomon built the temple, the stones used were made ready before it was brought to the building site so that there were no sound of axe or hammer or any other tool of iron heard in the house (1 Kings 6:7). We should understand that we are an important indispensable part of the great project to be commissioned soon as planned by the Almighty God. We are partakers in the building of the kingdom of God. "………But let every man take heed how he buildeth there upon………Know ye not that ye are the temple of God, and that the Spirit of God dwelleth in you?" (1 Corinthians 3:10-16). There may be confusions and doubts as to the fixing of right pieces in the right places. But those are to be cut or chiseled before bringing to the construction site. These confusions or hurdles on the way may appear in the form of small bickering, quarrels, resentments etc. That are to be resolved in a divine way for the sake of the fulfilment of the covenant obligation and love for each other (Ephesians 5:24-25). Let each partner and there by each family make themselves finely cut and polished stones for the building of God's kingdom.

St. Paul describes life as a race to be run steadfastly to win the crown. For a common man life usually represents married life. To win the crown we must finish the race successfully. It is cowardice to leave the arena or the pitch disobeying the rules of the game. The spirit of the marathon is in finishing the race as per rules and not in its good start. "Great beginnings are not important as great finishes".

Our race shall be lawful, as per rules, with patience, steadfastness etc., otherwise we may not be eligible for the crown. (2 Timothy 4:7-8, 2:5, Hebrews 12:1-2, 1 Corinthians 9:24.). Marriage life is a marathon - it is important to finish well and honor the marriage commitment made with God. It will be sinful if we fail in our commitment.

Let the Holy Spirit inspire married couples to assess and introspect their family life and make corrections wherever necessary for making Christian families role models in this "crooked and perverse nation …". Let the youths waiting for a married life have proper divine vision and wisdom about marriage and family life. Marriage is a relationship for each husband and wife to have and to hold forever, till the end of our life. God bless us.

8
Baptism

*B*aptism is accepted in most of the Christian churches as a sacrament and all believers are keen on observing the ritual even though in varying modes. During my childhood, it was just a ritual concerning the family only and it was done without much of a concern for others except the parents and grandparents and some close relatives, the priest, and officials of the church. It was performed after church worship, and everybody dispersed as usual to their homes. Time passed by and now it has become a subject for a great celebration whether the baptism is child baptism or adult baptism. I appreciate the change because it is worth celebrating ! St: Paul says, 'I am jealous for you with a godly jealousy. I promised you to one husband, to Christ, so that I might present you as a pure virgin to him' (NIV). Another version says, 'For I feel a divine jealousy for you, since I betrothed you to one husband, to present you as a pure virgin to Christ' (ESV). As marriage is an important ceremony in the life of a person betrothal is also to be celebrated in its importance. So, is in a way a baptismal ceremony. Whatever be the meaning we attribute to baptism or whatever be the manner we use for it, its culmination we see in the union of the church with Jesus Christ in his second advent. The baptized is admitted into the church, which we believe to be the bride. But the bride is the choice of the bridegroom from among the people all over the world without any consideration of the names given to the churches in this world or the baptismal procedure you go through.

We can see around three thousand Christian churches in this world. In each country umpteen number of Christian denominations are functioning. All these churches claim Jesus Christ as the capstone or the foundation of the church. Then, what is the subject for difference in the manner of worship and sacraments? Why should the churches accept things which are not specifically mentioned or taught by Jesus Christ and the apostles? Do they think that what Jesus taught is not sufficient to become the bride of him? Why do they change the truth of God into lies according to their own interpretations? Otherwise, I don't find any reason for the innumerable divisions among Christians.

The main difference between churches is in the sacraments which are the channels to receive God's grace to whom they are initiated or intended. There are differences in the number of sacraments in each church. Baptism is one among the three sacraments for initiation into the church – the body of Christ. The others are Confirmation and Eucharist or holy communion. Sacraments are supposed to confer Grace from the power of Holy Spirit believed to be present in the rites. The manner of performing baptism is one of the main subjects of controversy. If the convictions of each church are according to the word of God or revelations from God, why should there be confusions. Can anyone claim that the God who spoke to him/her is the real God, and the others are false preachers having no divine knowledge? Certain churches teach that the effect of baptism is spiritual regeneration which consists in the remission of every sin with the punishments due it, and the infusion of first grace. Some other churches accept baptism as only a sign of initiation into the membership of that church. Some others allow the church members to follow one's own conviction and administer baptism accordingly in the rituals. 'For God is not the author of confusion but of peace, as in all churches of the saints?' (1 Corinthians 14:33). Discussions are being conducted on various aspects of the ritual. Church leaders are trying to establish their conceptions to the believers who are less knowledgeable than them and tries to increase the number of lambs in their fold. Jesus says about such people addressing the lawyers of that period 'Woe unto you lawyers! For ye have taken away the key to knowledge; ye entered not in yourselves, and them that were entering in ye hindered' (Luke 11:52). We have to understand that baptism is not an issue at all, but faith is all that matters. Let us look into the Bible and come to a decision for ourselves. It is something personal to become the bride for Jesus Christ and is of no matter for the regional churches other than giving proper guidance as per the infallible word of God. In the present scenario we see that the church is concerned in its establishment and its maintenance. As during the period of Jesus even now most of the church leaders are corrupt. Most of them have fallen from their calling and vision. The leaders seem to have failed God like the pharisees, priests and scribes of the Jews.

Baptism in the Old Testament

Even though we cannot see the word baptism in the Old Testament English versions we see the word washing so many times. The word origin is in Greek *Baptizein/ Baptismos* and the OT being written in Hebrew we cannot see the word as such, and the word meaning being washing as an act of purification wherever we see an act of purification in the OT we can assume that all those instances point to an act of baptism. It includes washing, dipping, immersion, sprinkling etc. God directly gave those laws to his chosen people through Moses. We see it recorded that Moses did everything as God said. Moses obeyed God verbatim. There was no confusion in observing the laws. Punishments for disobedience of the law was also provided. Which was a deterrent for the people to obey it.

The books of Leviticus and Numbers deals with various kinds of washings for sanctifications. It includes rubbing, sprinkling, touching, washing in running water and immersing. It depends on the nature of sin or for specific purification requirements. Author of Hebrews refers it as '......... divers washings, and carnal ordinances, imposed on them until the time of reformation' (Hebrews 8:10). It was for a specific period up to the time of reformation. Those rituals were done externally, and it didn't have any influence on the inner being of people. Even though the laws were stringent the people still defiled the nation Israel and profaned the holy name of the Lord among the heathen. Through prophet Ezekiel, God reveals about a future day; 'Then will I sprinkle clean water upon you and ye shall be clean: from all your filthiness, and from all your idols, will I cleanse you. A new heart also will I give you, and a new spirit will I put within you: and I will take away the stony heart out of your flesh, and I will give you a heart of flesh ....' (Ezekiel 36:25-27). Pouring, sprinkling, immersing, and washing of any kind will give way to a new order that God has appointed when his "fullness of time" comes. 'This is the covenant I will make with the people of Israel after that time, declares the Lord. I will put my law in their minds and write it on their hearts. I will be their God, and they will be my people' (Jeremiah 31:33). Paul confirms the accomplishment of that covenant in his letter to Corinthians chapter 3. '.........written not with ink, but with the spirit of the living God., not in tables of stone, but in fleshy tables of the heart. And such trust have we through Christ to God-ward' (3:3-4).

Ministry of John the Baptist

It would be relevant to discuss briefly the backdrop of John's advent. His coming was prophesied by Isaiah and Malachi. (Isaiah 40:3, Malachi 3:1, 4:5-6).

After Malachi about 400 years Israel is seen to have no prophets to guide them. During this period different schools of thought emerged in various nations. Israel after the Babylonian exile could control Jerusalem and temple worships even though they were under the rule of different dynasties. They were ruled by Medo-Persia, Syria, Egypt, and Greeks. During the reign of Egypt under Ptolemy Hebrew Bible was translated to Greek and it was called *Septuagint* because the translation was done by seventy scholars. During the war campaigns of *Alexander, the great,* he gave more freedom to Israelites. This period had infiltrated great changes in the cultural and social life of the Jews. Jews spread among various countries started synagogues to worship even though temple of Jerusalem remained the main temple. Greek language began to be used as a common language. Greek philosophies also could have influenced their thoughts. There emerged various groups among Jews mainly Sadducees, Pharisees, Scribes, Essenes etc. interpreting and teaching the laws. They diluted the laws in many areas. Epicureans and Stoics were also influencing them. BC 160 to BC 63 Jerusalem was controlled by Maccabees and purification and rededication of the temple was done in this period. In BC 63 Romans came into power and then on, Jews were having very hard time. This was the time when John the Baptist started his ministry. It is no wonder he addressed those who came to him 'O, generation of vipers,' (Luke 3:7)

Purpose of John is to reveal the Messiah to Israel and to prepare the way of the Lord, to make his path straight. (Luke 3:4). It was his assignment as ordered by the Almighty to reveal the Messiah to Israel through the mode of water baptism. The generation of Israel was corrupt on one side and on the other they were in dire need of a redeemer. There were enough prophesies regarding the Messiah. John has declared that the kingdom they dreamed all these days is nigh and the prophesies are going to be fulfilled. "I am proclaiming the arrival of the Messiah. Get transformed to accept and believe him". He did not know who that anointed and appointed person was. The sign given to him was that while baptizing in water on whom you see the spirit coming down as a dove, he will be the son of God. 'And I knew him not: but that he should be made manifest to Israel, therefore am I come baptizing with water' (read John 1:31-34). The ministry of John must end as soon as the purpose is accomplished. '........ this my joy therefore is fulfilled. He must increase but I must decrease' (John 3:29-30).

New Testament

'But when the fullness of time was come, God sent forth his son, made of a woman, under the law, to redeem them that were under the law, that we might receive the adoption of sons' (Galatians 4:4-5).

Ministry of Jesus

Ministry of Jesus starts thence. Jesus after being baptized in water was taken to the wilderness to be tempted by Satan. Jesus started his ministry preaching repentance, for the kingdom of heaven is at hand. He began teaching the prophesies about the Messiah and the scriptures. He admonished the priests, pharisees and scribes for their wrong teachings and cleansed the temple. He healed the sick and gave life to the dead. He modelled a life of love and service. He shews that the love of God is manifest in loving others. Rather he *commanded* to love each other (John 13:34, 15:12). He exhorted them to serve others as he had done to them in washing their feet (John 13:14-15). He commanded to observe fellowship and communion (Luke 22:19). He taught how to worship God in spirit and truth. No aspect of human life he left untouched. He taught through parables. But he didn't baptize anyone or commanded to baptize while in mortal body in this world. He lived a loyal, sincere Jew observing the laws obeying God the father until he accomplished his ministry of becoming a sacrifice for the redemption of the world of its sins.

Peter

After the death and resurrection of Jesus Christ, getting confirmed in faith and receiving Holy Spirit, the disciples continued the ministry mainly among Jews. Peter seems to be the leader in spreading the Gospel during AD 30's onward. Peter is seen baptizing the gentiles who received the Holy Spirit in Caesarea. Peter is also seen addressing the assembly of disciples in Jerusalem (during AD 49/50) and conclude his speech by stating that the gentile converts shall not be insisted to follow Jewish religious tradition. The Jews of that time were following certain Jewish religious practices including baptism to mark conversion to Christian faith. In the initial stages of spreading the gospel it was the policy not to trouble the converts with many does and don'ts except for the four items agreed by the council of apostles. . Its outcome was " ….. we trouble not them, which from among the gentiles are turned to God: But that we write to them that they abstain from pollutions of idol, and from fornication, and from things strangled, and from blood".

Paul

Subsequently Paul comes into the scene and starts ministry among the gentiles. During the spread and progress of the church they faced many doubts from various corners regarding the manner of worship and rituals to be observed because even some Jews settled in other regions were under the grip of gentile worships prevailing in those countries and there were also gentiles turned to God and conservative Jews who insisted for the observation of Jewish rites. The confusion regarding the insistence of Jewish practices on the gentile converts was raised by Paul and Barnabas. In Paul's ministry we see that Paul is trying to convince the conservative Jews that the new covenant does not require the observation of the rites in the old covenant. The allowances given by the first assembly of apostles was to be discarded gradually as the believers come to a stage of knowledge of the Word of God. He vehemently states through his various epistles that the works of law must be done away with to become perfect in knowledge. The need of acquiring divine knowledge is stressed in most of his letters and preaching. From Peter's ministry toward the end of Paul's ministry we see this transition. Especially in the books of Hebrews and James we see the difference between the work of law and the works of faith. The Bible is called so because it has a perfect beginning a perfect progression and a perfect ending. Its books are arranged not chronologically but progressively towards a perfect ending

Apostles Creed

The Apostles Creed supposed to be written by twelve apostles, though there is no proof, but is the basic documented confession of faith and it turned to be a manual of the early Christian ministers.

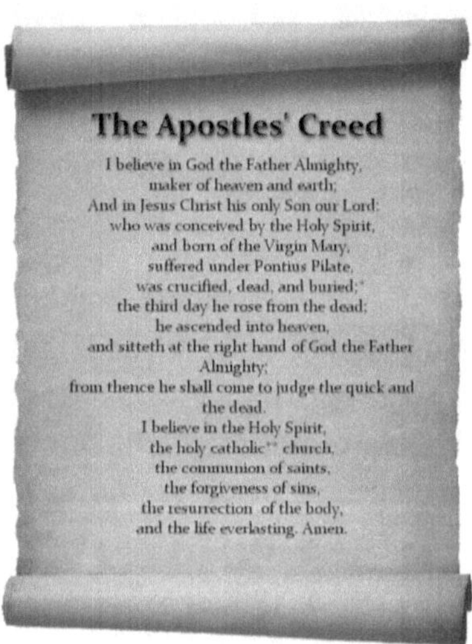

The source of the creed is supposed to be contributed by the Apostles, each contributing one article inspired by the Holy Spirit. It does not address many of the Christological or Theological issues which arose afterwards as the church spread to various countries and cultures. As there is no proof of this document being formulated by the Apostles, in the compilation of Bible later, this document is not included. Any how it may be taken for granted that among the early Christian groups this document made great influence in promulgating the various rites that have found its niche in church worships later. It is very clear from the writings of apostles which were compiled and included in the Bible that baptism was not anything restricted by the first Jerusalem Council and existed among the believers and the Jews simultaneously as its origin was the Mosaic Laws. Moreover, the influence of Jewish Christians was great among the believers. Also, we can see from the letters of Paul that he wants believers to attain perfection in divine knowledge. His letters aim at the transition of the believers from the works of law to the works of spirit. It is for the believers to grow in spirit and abandon those things that are unnecessary, unwanted, or unwarranted as per the gist of the gospel of the Kingdom of God

Didache

In the meanwhile, a creed (a formal statement of Christian beliefs) was formulated containing instructions regarding church order and the system of worship which is known as Didache also known as Lord's teachings or Teachings of the Apostles supposedly written by the end of first century or beginning of second century AD. Didache means 'by the Gospel' and is mainly attributed to the Gospel of Matthew. Even though the date of its origin is not known it is presumed to have been documented some time before the middle of the second century. It consists of a "Two Way" section which is said to be *"Christian redaction of a Jewish document"* about the way of life and the way of death, a liturgical manual, instructions on the travelling prophets and a brief apocalypse. **The Two Ways** material appears to have been intended as a summary of basic instruction about the Christian life to be taught to those who were preparing for baptism and church membership According to this text, thanksgiving prayer for the holy communion does not have a mention of the death and resurrection of Jesus Christ.

"We thank Thee, our Father, for the life and knowledge which Thou made known to us through Jesus Thy Servant; to Thee be the glory forever. Even as this broken bread was scattered over the hills and was gathered and became one, so let Thy Church be gathered together from the ends of the earth into Thy kingdom; for Thine is the glory and the power through Jesus Christ forever. But let no one eat or drink of your Eucharist, unless they have been baptized into the name of the Lord; for concerning this also the Lord has said, "Give not that which is holy to the dogs.". *"The prayers are for the food and drink created for all the people and the <u>special spiritual food and drink</u> that Christians have because of Jesus.*

Drinking the cup symbolizes the knowledge these people have that they and Jesus are the holy Vine of David which means that they belong to Israel. Eating the bread symbolizes the knowledge these people have of the life and immortality they enjoy by belonging to the Kingdom of God made known to them by Jesus God's child. No one is allowed to eat drink of your Eucharist except those who have been baptized in the Lord's name. ...... They continued to cultivate their roots in a Jesus movement where enlightenment ethics made much more sense than worship of Jesus as the crucified Christ and risen Son of God". -Burton Mack.

About baptism the Didache gives the following instructions:

1. Concerning Baptism, baptize in this way. After you have spoken all these things, (accepting and declaring the faith) baptize in the name of the Father, and of the Son, and of the Holy Spirit in running water.

2. If you do not have running water, baptize in other water. If you are not able to baptize in cold water, then in warm water.

3. If you do not have either, pour water three times on the head in the name of the Father, and of the Son, and of the Holy Spirit.

4. Before baptism the one baptizing and the one being baptized are to fast, and any others who are able. Command the one being baptized to fast beforehand a day or two.

Nicene Creed (first council of Constantinople AD 325)

It outlines the theological, dogmatic, and historical foundation upon which Christian faith is based. Baptism was not a subject in the original document compiled in AD 325 in the first Nicaean Council. It was included in AD 381 when certain confusions arose among the believers in accepting a second time, persons who renounced the faith after having been baptized once.

Difference between the Apostles Creed and the Nicene Creed is that: -

Apostles' creed can rightly be regarded as a true summary of Apostles faith. It was also a baptismal symbol, and it was recited before being baptized. Its authority arises from the fact that confession of faith was made only once and that is before baptism. It need not be repeated and again. Whereas the authority of Nicene creed is in that it was crafted by the two councils based on the extant faith documents, manuscripts of Gospels, writings of Apostles and certain practices.

The wording in Apostle's creed "he went to the hades "(This might be based on what is stated in Peters Gospel 1 chapter 3 verse 19) is avoided in the Nicene creed.

"I believe" is changed to "we believe" in the Nicene Creed. (I don't understand why this is changed and we still recite as such on every worship. Belief is a personal matter, and the church can only lead us to faith. But accepting faith and continuing in faith is purely a personal relationship with God)

The portions regarding the belief in Holy Ghost, and the one holy Catholic church and one baptism was included in the Nicacan Creed in the council of Constantinople in AD 381

From the fore going we can assume that when the ministries spread to different parts of the world among different cultures there popped up many differences not in basic faith but on unimportant matters. Baptism was not a matter of concern during those days because only persons accepting the faith who are of enough maturity to understand were baptized after confessing the Christian faith. Originally the manner of baptism also was not of concern. From the first ministry of John towards the end of the ministry of Paul we see the transition in the matter of faith- from the observation of rituals as a part of faith to acquiring divine knowledge. In the initial stages we see Jewish rites were existing among the converted

Jews. They were reluctant to give up them. We see circumcision and Jewish practices encouraged even by Peter. Paul asks him "…. why compellest thou the gentiles to live as do the Jews?" We see Timothy also getting circumcised before he was introduced into the ministry. Gentiles also might have continued their own rituals which did not go against the instructions of the First Jerusalem Council. In Corinth they had a custom of baptizing on behalf of the dead. Paul wants such practices to be discontinued. When Paul returned to Jerusalem completing his missionary journeys, he was persuaded by the disciples to observe the laws on behalf of four men under a vow as per the Laws to convince the Jews that he also observes Jewish laws and is not against it. Such practices prevailed among Jewish Christians also (Acts 21:20-25). Author of the book of Hebrews lists out such practices as dead works and exhorts the Jews to go on unto perfection of faith toward God (Hebrews 6:1-2). Customs and rituals shall not form a part of our faith. It is written "Of how much sorer punishment, suppose ye, shall he be thought worthy, who hath trodden underfoot the Son of God, and hath counted the blood of covenant, wherewith he was sanctified, an unholy thing, and hath done despite unto the Spirit of Grace?" (Hebrews 10:29)

During the passage of time discussions continued these dead works as against the biblical instructions and churches began to split into various units on their own interpretations of the "dead works". The important subject of controversy is Baptism. Why should we try to explain baptism apart from Bible? We accept the Old Testament as shadow of the things to come. We always interpret biblical subjects in its spiritual aspects. The flood and redemption of Noah and family and the redemption of Israel from Egypt and their journey through the desert and red sea are all alluded as examples of Baptism. We have to interpret what baptism is, and how it is to be administered, or what its importance is, in the light of various washings mentioned in the Mosaic Laws, and the examples which are given spiritual meanings in the New Testament, and the contexts where it is done, or the words wash or baptize are used. The word is used to refer washing by immersion, submersion, dipping, sprinkling, pouring and ablution. Whatever the manner or meaning attributed by each church or group be, my belief is that Jesus and Apostle Paul are of the same opinion which most of the churches are ignoring. Jesus did not baptize anyone, and Paul states I have come not to baptize but to preach the Gospel. Then why should there be much uproar about baptism. Let it be aspersion, affusion or immersion what difference is it as it is not the means for spiritual transformation. Some churches see baptism as a sacrament, a means of grace from God and some other church consider it as an ordinance, a practice to demonstrate one's faith, some others consider it as a symbol of initiation into the church. Those who consider baptism as an ordinance say these rituals are outward expressions of faith, an outward witnessing of an inner reality. Anyhow there is no consensus among believers even as to the purpose of baptism.

Jesus Commanded it?

Jesus' ministry continued for three and a half years in this world. He was called Master and Rabbi. He taught the disciples and people that followed him everything necessary to enter the Kingdom of God and to receive heavenly blessing while in this world. He taught how to pray, how to worship, how to give charity, service, fellowship and to love God and brothers and neighbors and what more. He didn't teach how to baptize. What a paradox. He did not ask anyone to get baptized. When he sent his twelve disciples the first time with a mission, he did not command them to baptize. They were commanded to preach, with certain conditions as to their area of operation, that the Kingdom of Heaven is at hand and get transformed of your mind, and they were equipped with blessings and boons to pass on to the needy, freely. The same was the case when seventy disciples were sent with the mission of preaching. The baptism in water that was commanded to John is not continued by Jesus. He told the leper after he was healed to go to the priest and do what the law insists. He told the blind man to go and wash in the pool of Siloam. To no one else He seems to have told to do anything or get baptized for their complete recovery. And He told the people around to untie Lazarus when he was risen from the tomb. The Jewish Law and the contexts necessitated such instructions.

The verses in Matthew 28 and Mark 16 are quoted by them who argue for baptism to support their claim. Matthew and Mark are not the only persons who described the last days of Jesus in this world and His resurrection. Was John and Luke against the idea of Baptism for they have not mentioned it in their writings? In John's account about the last encounters with Jesus, John says that Jesus had breathed on them and said," receive ye the Holy Ghost". In my opinion this verse is more important than the ones in Mathew and Mark because John the Baptist said about Jesus that he will baptize in Holy Spirit. In the Gospel of John there is an affidavit also submitted in the last portion that "this is the disciple which testifieth of these things and wrote these things; and we know that his testimony is true". The baptism Mathew and Mark wrote must be a reference to this baptism of the Holy Ghost. "He that believeth and is baptized shall be saved: but he that *believeth not* shall be damned". Here belief is the core of the subject and not baptism. The Great Commission is, preaching the Gospel and making disciples for Christ, transforming many for the Kingdom of God. It is likely that baptism being a requirement for Judaizers to convert a person to Jewish community that was practiced as per Mosaic laws, the early Apostles might have used it for accepting a person to the faith. Water baptism was not a new thing brought by John the Baptist for persons on repenting and accepting the gospel of the Kingdom. Mark being a Jew might have been referring to spiritual baptism projecting the erstwhile extant processes used for conversions among Jews. [Moreover, in chapter sixteen of Mark verses from nine to twenty are said to be not seen in certain original manuscripts of the Gospel and it was added later}. When we analyze the confession of John the Baptist which goes like this '…. But he that sent me to baptize with water, the same said unto me, upon whom thou shalt see the Spirit descending, and remaining on him, *the same is he which baptizes with the Holy Ghost*' (John 1:33). Then how can Jesus' command something the Father has not expected him to do. Jesus who came to baptize in Holy Spirit can only command the baptism in spirit and not water. This contention is supported by Luke also in the first chapter of Acts. Jesus is stated to have stayed about forty days in the world and has manifested himself to the disciples making things clearer to them about the Kingdom of God. Jesus asks them not to move away from Jerusalem and wait there for the promise of the Father. He again specifically states that "For John truly baptized with water, but you shall be baptized with the Holy Ghost not many days hence". There are no contradictions in statements if we reasonably evaluate the prophecy of John about Jesus and the statements made by Jesus before and after resurrection. The baptism Jesus commanded is not of water for he has mentioned about the baptism of John emphatically here. When Jesus on the cross says everything is fulfilled, he is saying that the prophesies are fulfilled, and the Laws are complied with for all and forever. The laws written on stone is completely replaced by the new covenant written on the hearts. It is unambiguously stated in all the epistles and gospels. Why should we again bring the old Jewish "*Mikveh*" to our Christian domain.

[Mikveh is a pool of water in which the person who converts to Judaism is immersed to actualize his/her total transition from the old identity to his or her new identity as a Jew. This immersion is the core component of Jewish conversion process of any person man or woman, child, or adult, ignorant or scholarly, it is said].

For more evidence we may refer to Luke 12:50 where Jesus says, 'But I have a baptism to be baptized with…' and Mark 10:39 '….

And ye shall indeed drink of the cup that I drink of; and with the baptism that I am baptized withal shall ye be baptized'. How can we explain it? What is the baptism Jesus referring? It was nothing but his crucifixion and resurrection. He did not mention that I have another baptism, but I have a baptism. The only baptism that Jesus was concerned was his transformation to the heavenly body which was prophesied by David (Acts 2:31, Psalms 16:10). Moreover, it does not conform to logic that Jesus would command something which he has not done or told to be done while in this world he would command to his disciple to do after his resurrection. The only one baptism referred in the Nicaean creed is this baptism Jesus mentioned and not a water baptism, I strongly believe.

The **Great Commandment** is a name used in the New Testament to describe the first of two commandments given by Jesus in Matthew 22:35–40, Mark 12:28–34 and Luke 10:27.

In Mark, when asked "which is the great commandment in the law?", Jesus answered, 'Hear, O Israel! The Lord Our God, The Lord is One; Thou shalt love thy Lord, thy God with all thy heart, and with all thy soul, and with all thy mind', 'And the second is like unto it, thou shalt love thy neighbor as thyself'. Most Christian denominations consider these two commandments to be the core of Christian living.

The **Golden Rule** is the principle of treating others as you want to be treated. It is a maxim that is found in many religions and cultures It can be considered an **ethic of reciprocity** in some religions, although different religions treat it differently.

Jesus prays to God in His intercessory prayer 'I gave them the words you gave me, and they accepted them ………' John 17:8. While in this world Jesus gave through his disciples all that the father gave him. Did he miss to say about baptism? Or did the father give the additional instruction after resurrection. Can we say that Jesus forgot to say about water baptism, so he said it after resurrection?

Jesus was baptized, so his followers also should get baptized.

Jesus was circumcised does it mean that followers from gentiles should also do that. Maria took him to the temple along with the sacrificial dove for her purification and dedication of child. The laws given to Jews through Moses were to be obeyed and observed by the Jews. Jesus came under that law, and he has to obey those laws. Along with this argument some people also argue that to be righteous before the Lord, baptism is compulsory. This is based on the verse in Matthew '…. to fulfill all righteousness…' (3:15). Jesus said this about being loyal to the God given laws because the water baptism of John the Baptist was ordained by God. It is written "But the pharisees and lawyers rejected the counsel of God against themselves, being not baptized of him". When Paul writes to the Galatians it is specifically stated that "But when the fullness of time was come, God sent forth his son, made of a woman, *made under the law*". Being baptized in water, Jesus was first, under the compulsion of law of God and second, for the purpose that he is to be revealed to Israel and to be witnessed by John that Jesus is the Messiah. That was the intention of the baptism in water of John. John's message and the message of Jesus both were that the Kingdom of God is near and get transformed and turn to God. John also declared that he who comes after me will baptize you in Holy Spirit and fire. The assignment of Jesus also is to pass judgement on those who do not accept the baptism of Holy spirit. "Whose fan is in his hand, and he will thoroughly purge his floor, and will gather the wheat into his garner, but the chaff he will burn with fire unquenchable". (Luke 3:17). The law of external works for becoming righteous ends with the new covenant of God entered with all humans through the blood of Jesus. "This cup is the New Testament in my blood, which is shed for you". The New Testament comes into effect on the death of the executor of the law. It is prophesied many times that there shall come a new covenant for Israel and all world. The first testament was not faultless, and it was a covenant based on the promise of

God to Abraham. The covenant that God gave through Moses was for the nation of Israel – the children of Abraham. When we say of a *New Testament* the old is completely replaced by it. 'Then he said, Lo, I come to do thy will, O, God. He taketh away the first that he may establish the second' (Hebrews 10:9). The promises given in the Old Testament are for Israel the nation. We have got more precious and blessed promises. We see in the Old Testament promises about material possessions and provisions for protections against enemies and destruction of the enemies of Israel. The New Testament does not offer destruction of the enemies rather wants us to love our enemies too. The effect of the new covenant is seeing heavenly glory when being stoned to death or receiving God's revelation when isolated and starved. This new vine is to be stored in the new wineskin the transformed hearts. We must be careful not to add the old vine also into the revived hearts. If we do so it would amount to considering the blood of Jesus unholy or not sufficient for salvation. We are despising the spirit of grace. Anything done on our body to swagger as the Jews boasted on circumcision will not do any good for our salvation. Jesus accepted water baptism as ordained by God because he came to fulfill the laws. Anyone accepting the gift of salvation by faith is not expected to do any works of law or any external washings or ablutions to complement salvation. Christ will become of no effect for those who try to become justified through the Mosaic Laws. They are "fallen from grace" (Galatians 5:2-5).

The concept of Sacred time and Ordinary time prevail in certain churches. *"Sacred time is not concerned at all with the sequence of events in ordinary time. Ordinary time is the succession of moments in history. The concern of Sacred time lies in the salvific content and meaning of the event or events that take place either in the primordial time, in the beginning or at a point or points in the historical time. These salvific events continue to be effective throughout history and can be recaptured at any point in historical time since they are eternally present in Sacred time. Eg: The entry into Sacred time takes place primarily in the eucharist (Holy Communion) liturgy. Each Sunday becomes in sacred time the day of resurrection. The entry into sacred time is effectuated by the Holy Spirit. At the time of praying to bless the elements during the holy communion it is believed that the bread and vine turns to flesh and blood of Jesus Christ. Likewise, at the consecration of the baptismal font the water becomes the Jordan water into which Jesus Christ was baptized. In both Eucharist and Baptism, a salvific event in the life of Christ is re-presented, by means of the conjunction of Sacred time- the eternal now – with that moment in historical time at which the liturgical action takes place. This is brought about by the Holy Spirit making the "not yet" into the "already"".* This concept is accepted in certain churches. They believe that the baptismal water turns into the water of Jordan river in which Jesus was baptized. This thinking is of no foundation in the word of God and is not accepted by protestant churches.

Can baptism bring salvation?

"To put it most simply, the power, effect, benefit, fruit, and purpose of Baptism is to save ……. To be saved, we know, is nothing else than to be delivered from sin, death and the devil and to enter into the kingdom of Christ and live with him forever" – Martin Luther

I disagree with his observations if only it denotes to water baptism, for the following reasons.

'And now why tarriest thou? Arise and be baptized, and wash away thy sins, calling on the name of the Lord' (Acts 22:16). Ananias was appointed by the Lord to enquire about Saul and then put hand on him so that he regains sight. Ananias testifies this to Saul that Jesus has sent me so that you may receive sight and be filled with the Holy Ghost. Ananias was a disciple from the gentiles in Damascus and Saul a Jew. Saul was so far against the Christian faith till then. Believers in Damascus were in fear of Saul as he had reached there to slaughter or drag the believers to the high priest. As for Ananias who was directed by the Lord and for Saul it was desired to confirm his transformation, water baptism was administered by the then prevailing custom. God already accepted Saul as an apostle for the gentiles and for sufferings on behalf of the Kingdom of God. His old views have changed, and a new vision and holy spirit was given to him even before being baptized. This same Paul when he grows further in his ministry establishes through his various writings that no works external to the body can bring in salvation. Water baptism does not have any salvific effect and in washing away the sins. About John the Baptist it is seen written that "John did baptize in the wilderness and preach the baptism of repentance for the remission of the sins." Remission of sins is through repentance and repentance is also called baptism here. It is a purification by submergence in Spirit. The Jews who so far had been doing works of the law cannot easily accept the idea of just repenting for washing away the sins, but they want some signs or actions of their part. For every religious community or even person it would be difficult to change to a new pattern of behavior or system of faith immediately without any actions from their part. Hence, we understand that a period for the transition is necessary to clear away certain beliefs and practices we have been following and replace it with certain new ideologies and principles especially in religious realm. Towards the last chapters of the bible, we can see this progressive transition. The book of Hebrews strongly opposes any physical activities for salvation. New Testament is not an add on to the old one and it is the complete replacement of the old. Old Testament serves as a study tool for the history of Israel and Gods functioning through the ages and evidence for Gods works on nations and humans and the nature of God.

Now most of the churches accept that water baptism is not a *sine qua non* for Salvation. Salvation is the gift of God bestowed on those who believe in the only begotten son of God, Jesus Christ. Even when we were dead in sins, he has quickened us together with Christ and by *grace* we are saved. *It is the gift of*

God. No works of law is needed. (Ephesians 2:4-10). Again, Paul says "… by setting aside in his flesh the law with its commands and regulations". All the works of the law are dispensed with by the sacrifice of Jesus on the cross. The practices observed by the Jews are not for the gentiles to be observed. Cross is the only way for all to get reconciled to God. Further, we must understand the difference between redemption and salvation. Redemption is a onetime activity of accepting Jesus Christ as our savior and redeemer, the shadow of which we see in the OT is the Passover of the Israelites from the bondage of Pharaoh by the blood of the lamb. The process of salvation is the journey through the wilderness up to the entry into Canaan. Canaan life is the true Christian life as Paul says, "Christ is living in me". Jordan is the transformation to the new life with Jehova, that is our assurance and confirmation of our salvation. In Canaan we must face and endure sufferings and hardships. Their new life started from there. A state where we must exercise our faith and loyalty to our savior, and the Lord will transform us into the likeness of Jesus Christ. To become partakers of his sufferings. The perfection of our salvation is yet to come. The faithful believers of the past as described in Hebrew 11 and the first part of chapter 12 are still waiting for it. The reason is we the present-day believers are to join with them in the perfection of salvation. The believers of the old and New Testament together will come to the perfection of salvation. We must seriously think of how they came to this confirmation of their faith in their life. They endured sufferings! That was their baptism, not anything less.

When we recite our faith as per the Nicene creed, we confirm that there is only one baptism for salvation. Which is that one and only baptism mentioned there? Let us turn to Luke 12:50 where we see Jesus saying, "I have a baptism to undergo". If this baptism refers to the sufferings of Jesus and his death on cross for the salvation of the humankind, that alone is the baptism for every human being for salvation. Let us view this verse together with Hebrew 10:29 which reads thus "How much more severely do you think someone deserves to be punished who has trampled the Son of God underfoot, who has treated as an unholy thing the blood of the covenant that sanctified them, and who has insulted the Spirit of grace?" (NIV). 'For if when we were enemies we were reconciled to God *through the death of His Son*, much more, having been reconciled, *we shall be saved by His life*. And not only that, but we also rejoice in God through our Lord Jesus Christ, through whom we have now received the reconciliation'. (Romans 5:10) If so, what is the relevance of baptism in water. Some people say it is an act of obedience.

Act of obedience?

We have already seen that the concept of water baptism as a command is a mis- conception of facts considering the context and the biblical message in its entirety. Mark is supposed to be the first gospel among the synoptic gospels. Main source of information for Matthew is said to be from Mark with some additional information. Mark was neither a disciple nor a follower of Jesus. He is seen joining Paul in his ministry. His gospel might have been written from the information received from Paul and Apostles. The gospel of John is the last written gospel, and it differs much from the contents in the other gospels. The differences in these Gospels need not be considered as contradictions. "*These books do not claim to be objective histories; they claim to be proclamation of good news*". So, the incidents and events cannot be historically accurate. These books proclaim information about Jesus and his teachings which are meant for salvation. He who believes in the only begotten son should have everlasting life. God gave the power to become sons of God to those who believe in Jesus Christ. Advocates for baptism argue that Jesus said to Nicodemus 'except a man be born of water and of the spirit, he cannot enter into the Kingdom of God'. But in the next sentence it is seen written that which is born of the flesh is flesh and which is born of the spirit is spirit. I strongly believe that the water Jesus said is the water of life, The Word of God, that

Jesus told to the woman of Samaria. ' .... The water that I shall give him shall be in him a well of water springing up into everlasting life'. If we do not understand the true meaning of what Jesus said and what the Bible says, it is woe to us. There are other commands and exhortations that Jesus gave to the disciples specifically. Do we obey them? 'If ye keep my commandments ye shall abide in my love .... *This is my commandment*, that ye love one another, as I have loved you'. And again, Jesus says '...... *for all things that I have heard of my Father I have made known unto you'* (John 15:15). Paul says towards the end of his ministry that after I leave this world there will arise false teachers (word used is - savage wolves) to deceive you. They will distort the truth in order to draw away disciples after them. Jesus too had warned against such false teachers. From the last phase of the first century itself we can see differences of opinions arising in the early churches, mainly because of the influence of various philosophical thinking of that period and of the various other writings supposedly written by other disciples and authors during that time. Jesus exhorted his disciples to serve one another as he has shown by washing their feet. He broke his body for the sin of the world and symbolized it by breaking the bread and exhorted the disciples to observe the same in their life. Share your body and bread with your brethren. These are the fruits expected from the redeemed and saved people. Do we bear these fruits for the benefit of others? The Word is clear to us in all matters to be obedient to God 'Therefore, brothers and sisters, since we have confidence to enter the most Holy Place by the *blood of Jesus, by the new and living way opened for us through the curtain, that is his body*, and since we have a great priest over the house of God let us draw near to God with a sincere heart and with the full assurance that faith brings, having our hearts sprinkled to cleanse us from a guilty conscience and having our bodies washed with pure water'(Hebrews 11: 19-25). The activities of our body shall be in accordance with the Word of God. Pure water represents the living water Jesus offered to the woman of Samaria. We are obeying God when we do the works of faith.

Baptism identifies us with Christ and the Church?

'Know ye not, that so many of us as were baptized into Jesus Christ were baptized into his death' (Romans 6:3). Jesus said, 'He that hath my commandments, and keeping them, he is that loveth me; and he that loveth me shall be loved of my Father, and I will love him, and will manifest in him'. Jesus manifesting in a person is the ultimate hope of a Christian when living in this world. 'But we all with open face beholding as in a glass the Glory of the Lord, are changed into the same image from glory to glory, even as by the spirit of the Lord' (2 Corinthians 3:18). It is the work of the spirit that transform us into to the image of Jesus Christ and not water. 'Now if any man has not the spirit of Christ, he is none of His' (Romans 8:9). All these verses confirm that Holy Spirit is doing the work of getting us reconciled and united to God. The Holy Spirit working in our human spirit is responsible for the thinking of the mind and performance of the body in a Christian believer. 'And the very God of peace sanctify you wholly; and I pray God your whole **Spirit and Soul and Body** be preserved blameless unto the coming of our Lord Jesus Christ' (1 Thessalonians 5:23). This is the order in a true believer in his life pattern starting from the Holy Spirit dwelling in our human spirit and taking control of our lives.And that is the signature of God in a man to be revealed to the public.

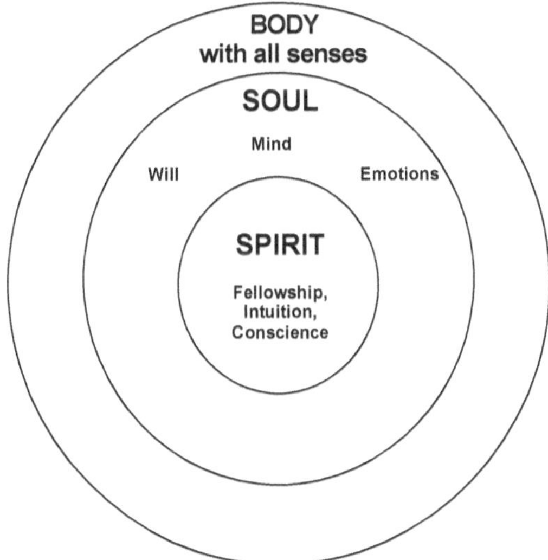

Figure: The Triune identity of Man, as per Bible

SPIRIT – Human spirit becomes one with the spirit of Christ.

Attributes are Fellowship,Intuition and Conscience

SOUL – Mind, Will and Emotions

BODY – With all senses

He who is in the flesh cannot please God. Carnal mind is enmity to God. His mind and spirit are designed and directed by worldly pleasures. Many religious thoughts are based on controlling body first, then the soul and then get identified with God in one spirit. *Yoga Marga* is one of the ways to get one with God in the Hindu dharma.

'Physical training is of some value but godliness has value for all things, holding promise for both the present life and the life to come' (1 Timothy 4:8). 'His divine power has given us everything we need for a godly life through our knowledge of Him who called us by his own glory and goodness'. We need to acquire first the knowledge of Jesus Christ to get identified with him. We see many Christians are dragged towards luxuries, power, and positions of this world. 'Godliness with contentment is great gain' (1 Timothy 6:6). They have lost their visions. They are of corrupt minds, and destitute of the truth.

The concept that when we immerse in water it symbolizes the burial of Jesus and when we rise from water it symbolizes the resurrection of Jesus and thus, we are becoming united or joined to Jesus is only a weak and meaningless thought in my opinion. We are not expected to start with the flesh again and try to end in spirit, when we accept Jesus Christ as our Lord and Savior, because it will not succeed. Our way is starting our Christian life in Spirit as the first gift of grace is the spirit of God, and then submitting our whole life to Jesus Christ to follow him as he has been an example for us. Jesus submitted himself to be sacrificed after great torture and sufferings. Bible says we must go through his hardships in order to be partakers of his resurrection. Then, are we ready to suffer for him to get identified with him? That is what the new covenant wants of us to get identified with his resurrection." ...., That I may **know him**, and the power of **his resurrection**, and the **fellowship of his sufferings**, being made **conformable unto his death**, if by any means I might attain **unto the resurrection** of the dead". Shall we accept what Paul says as the right way to become one with Jesus in our lives and count everything other than the cross of Jesus as dung, if we have a shortcut to become one with God through water baptism? To understand these things the excellency of the knowledge of Christ Jesus is required. We should not be of the spiritual level of Nicodemus when he asked Jesus "can we enter the second time into our mother's womb and be born?" It is ridiculous to evaluate what is spiritual with human knowledge. Jesus when he asked his disciples "Can you drink the cup I drink or be baptized with the baptism I am baptized with?" he was giving them a warning that they too are going to be identified with him in his sufferings and a baptism in spirit. "We can" they answered. Jesus said to them," You will drink the cup I drink and be baptized with the baptism I am baptized with". Not a water baptism for them to get identified with Jesus. 'For by one spirit are we all baptized into one body, ……… and have been all made to drink into one spirit' (1 Corinthians 12:13). This is what is to say about all the believers being the parts of one body the church. 'One Lord, one faith, one baptism ….'. (Ephesians 4:5). What is this one baptism talked about, that is declared through the Nicene creed also. That is the baptism Jesus said, The Cross. Those who believed and saved were added to the church by the Lord. Church is the gathering of those who are saved by faith and not of them that are baptized in water. When we say we are baptized into one body it is the one baptism we accept, that is of the Holy Spirit, when we believe in the cross and resurrection of our Lord, are we not believing that we are regenerated into a life with the resurrected Jesus Christ. Jesus prays to the Father, 'My prayer is not for them alone, I pray also for those who will ***believe in me through their message***, that all of them may be one, Father just as you are in me and I am in you, ***may they also be in us*** so that the world may believe that you have sent me' (John 17:20-21). Believing in Jesus Christ makes us one with God through Him. Not baptism. 'The cup of blessing which we bless, is it not the communion of the blood of Christ? The bread which we break, is it not the communion of the body of Christ? For we being many are one bread, and one body; for we are all partakers of that one bread.' (1 Corinthians 10:16-17). Jesus said, 'this is my body which is given for you: do this in remembrance of me'. When we too are willing to share our body and all that God has given us, then we too become identical with Jesus, of the same character of Jesus. 'He that eats my flesh, and drinks my blood, dwells in me, and I in him'(John 6:56).He is the one that has descended from heaven; the bread of life and the Word that became flesh. Eating His flesh is imbibing the word of God and living by it.

Baptism is a symbol of New Life – a statement of faith

We can say circumcision is a symbol of God's covenant to the nation of Israel or the children of Abraham. 'For in Christ Jesus neither circumcision availeth anything, nor uncircumcision, but a new creature' (Galatians 6:15). If the rite of circumcision is done away with for the New Testament people, what could it be of water baptism which does not make any mark on the person receiving it. The symbol that identifies a true believer is fruit of the Spirit produced by him. As for witnessing one's faith, what difference it makes if not baptized in water and declares his faith in public. Moreover, none of these are witnessed by anyone other than the church members and relatives. What effect the water baptism makes on the baptized and the on lookers. It goes just as a customary rite of the church. To be a member of the Church of our Lord, "put on the new man, which after God is created in righteousness and true holiness". Bear the fruits of spirit. 'Therefore, leaving the principles of the doctrine of Christ, let us go on **unto perfection**; not laying again the foundation of repentance from **dead works**, and of faith toward God, of the doctrine of baptisms, and laying of hands and of resurrection of the dead, and of eternal judgement' (Hebrews 6:1-2). We are ignorant of the depth of these verses. Whoever be the author of this book a great philosophy is involved in these remarks. Jesus have shown us a **way of life** saying he is the way the truth and life. He did not say I am teaching you the way, truth, and life. But he **is** it. That we must understand and manifest in us. Living the life Jesus has modelled for us is our actual Christian life, let us be of the same character of Jesus. That is what is expected of us. It is already time to reflect the image of Jesus in our lives. The main reason that the Old Testament people failed is that they wanted to live according to the law in its literal meaning rejecting the spirit of it. And accordingly, their lifestyle

> *"If we are truly in love with Christ and if we sense how much he loves us, our hearts will light up with a joy that spreads to everyone around us"*
>
> *– quote*

was based on how far they can live even sinfully without affecting the law. To what extend their freedom can be utilized for their own benefits without infringing the laws. They interpreted the law to their favor. Jesus reveals their disloyalty and infidelity saying '…. For ye pay tithe of mint and anise and cumin, and have omitted the weightier matters of the law, judgement, mercy, and faith; ………… Ye blind guides, which strain at a gnat, and swallow the camel' (Matthew 23:23-24). This should not happen to the New Testament believers. Unnecessary customs and rites in the name of basic matters shall not form part of our faith and life. In the book of Job, we see a statement of Zophar, 'Can you fathom the mysteries of God? Can you probe the limits of the Almighty?' (Job 11:7). During those periods people could not think of a God who will punish a righteous man with sufferings. That was the circumstances the Old Testament people were living in. Their thoughts were mainly rationalized according to the law which was providing for their physical existence only. Jesus revealed the Almighty God to us through him and his plans for man is made explicit for us. Paul made it obvious that the Old Testament was guiding us toward a new system based on faith only. 'Before the coming of this faith we were held under the law, locked up until the faith that was to come would be revealed. So, the law was our guardian until Christ came that we might be justified by faith. Now, that this faith has come, we are no longer under a guardian' (Galatians 3:23-25). The law of the flesh has given way to a law of the Spirit. If we are in Spirit, we can discern God's mysteries. 'The person without the Spirit does not accept the things that come from the spirit of God but considers them foolishness and cannot understand them because they are discerned only through the spirit ……. but we have the spirit of Christ' (1 Corinthians 2:14-16). Pour new wine into new wineskins so that both will be preserved. When we say we are New Testament people display our newness in our renewed life pattern according to the New Testament with no additions or deletions.

The transition from Old Testament to New Testament we have to understand: -

From under law till John's ministry →Jesus →Peter →Paul

Jews →Gentiles

 Nation of Israel →Church, the Believers

Water →Word of God, Flesh →Spirit

Signs →Faith

'His divine power has given us everything we need for a godly life **through our knowledge of Him** who called us by his own glory and goodness' (2 Peter 1:3). Then what is the significance of an immediately fading act to represent the transformation of the mind. I don't understand the rationale behind it. Somebody said of water baptism as a public testimony of a private experience. Paul says about the Israelites who are still observing the Law 'For I bear them record that they have a zeal of God, but not according to knowledge' (Romans 10:2). Whatever be the reason attributed for water baptism nothing can justify it because 'If thou shalt confess with thy mouth the Lord Jesus, and shalt **believe in thine heart** that God hath raised him from the dead, thou shalt be saved .... '(Romans 10:9-10). Believing in truth and spirit brings redemption, justification, salvation, and glorification, then what more we receive by water baptism. To me it is beyond my logic and reasoning, excuse. Why should Paul thank God for not baptizing anyone other than certain named ones. He also says Christ sent him to preach Gospel and not to baptize. (1 Corinthians 1:14, 17). They preached and won disciples. Are we becoming more loyal to Christ adding something which Jesus had not done himself and Paul rejects to do it anymore? It was there till the time of reformation. Rites done on flesh were the shadow of the good things to come. When the real things have come why should we again go behind the shadow. When we try to preach the word with our own wisdom clinging to the literal meaning of words without understanding the totality of the word of God given to us through the New Testament, amounts to disparaging the cross of Christ. 'Therefore, if anyone is in Christ, the new creation has come; the old has gone, the new is here.' (2 Corinthians 5:17)

To Receive Holy Ghost?

There is an incident reported in the book of Acts that of Paul meeting some disciples in Ephesus. Paul asks them whether they have received the Holy Ghost. They say no. They were baptized in the name of Lord Jesus and when Paul laid his hands upon them the Holy Ghost came upon them. These people were already baptized in water, that is they received John's baptism. But they didn't receive the Spirit, even they haven't heard of Holy Spirit. I find no reason to believe that they were again given a baptism in water. Here the baptism represents their transformation hearing the true gospel of Jesus and the gift of Holy spirit. Holy Spirit is the first fruit of our belief, it is the first divine gift for the believer. Here the water baptism they received earlier was not of any use. And the same is the case even now. Repentance of our sin on believing that Jesus had made the recompense for our sins, washes us of any blemishes in our life and sanctifies and justifies us once for all. This washing is referred as baptism in the New Testament in its reality. The term baptism is generic in nature, and it does not mean water baptism only wherever it is seen in the NT.

In the house of Cornelius, we see Peter preaching to the gentiles gathered in that house. 'While Peter yet spake these words, the Holy Ghost fell on all of them which heard the word. .... And they of the circumcision which believed were astonished, as many as came with Peter, ...and he commanded them to be baptized in the name of the Lord' (Acts 10:44-48). Here the context is very important. Peter was followed by Jews who, even after coming to faith want Water baptism as a sign of conversion. It was demanded by the Jews that those who received Holy Ghost shall be baptized in water. Moreover, Peter was an Apostle of the Jews, and he was an advocate for Jewish rites. He had been compelling the Gentiles to live like Jews. As Paul said the Jews seek signs for faith but the Greeks seek worldly wisdom, but both are futile. Wisdom from above is needed to discern heavenly things. Even though Peter remembers what Jesus told them before ascension, that John gave you water baptism, but you will be baptized with Holy Ghost sooner, he gave a command for water baptism in fear of the Jews that followed him. Water baptism was given to those who received the baptism of the spirit. Similar situation we see in the case of Timothy also. He was circumcised for fear of the Jewish Christians. Baptism came after receiving Holy Spirit. The Word was the cause for receiving Holy Spirit. What is the significance of that water baptism? "Now ye are clean through the word which I have spoken unto you" (John 15:3). Jesus said it. Water symbolizes the Word in the Bible. Because consecration is effectuated by the Word of God and prayer (1 Timothy 4:5). Again, about this incident Peter witnesses before the council of Apostles.

But we believe that through the grace of the Lord Jesus Christ we shall be saved, even as they (Acts 15:11). Holy Spirit is the first fruit that a person receives from God when he believes in His heart, Jesus Christ is his savior and God, and he witnesses it through his mouth. All the divine blessings follow it. Paul asks the Galatian "this only would I learn of you, Received ye the Spirit by the works of the law or by hearing of faith?" We too must answer that question. Water baptism was a work of the law that was assigned to John in the periods of the OT and with a specific purpose.

Galatians 6: 8 'For he that soweth to his flesh shall of the flesh reap corruption: but he that soweth to the spirit shall of the spirit reap life everlasting....12. As many as desire to make a fair shew in the flesh, they constrain you to be circumcised; only lest they should suffer persecution for the cross of Christ......14. But God forbid, that I should glory, save in the cross of our Lord Jesus Christ, by whom the world is crucified unto me, and I unto the world. 15.

For in Christ Jesus neither circumcision nor uncircumcision, but a new creature'. We must bear the mark of the Lord Jesus in our body, the indelible mark and not the delible one of baptism.

Apostle James warns 'Not many of you should become teachers, my fellow believers, because you know that we who teach will be judged more strictly. We all stumble in many ways …. '. No man can lay a foundation other than the one which is Jesus Christ. If the Spirit of God is dwelling in us, we cannot build on that foundation with any mean things such as gold, silver, stones, wood, hay, straw etc. and make a Christian group. It may amount blind leading the blind.

The word of God itself is the warp and woof for the study of the bible. We should observe the laws of **hermeneutics** i.e. The laws of interpretation of Bible in conveying the mysteries underlying each verse in the Bible. We should study every verse in its context, cross reference, language, historical and cultural back grounds.'For the wisdom of this world is foolishness before God. For it is written he is the **one who catches the wise in their craftiness** and again **the Lord knows the reasonings of the wise that they are useless** '(1 Corinthians 3:19-20). We cannot interpret the bible according to our human knowledge. Only the spirituals can understand what is written by the inspiration of the Holy Spirit. 'So then, just as you received Christ Jesus as Lord, continue to live your lives in him, *rooted and built up in him, strengthened in faith as you were taught*, and overflowing with thankfulness'. (Colossians 2:6-7). 'His divine power has given us everything we need for a godly life through our knowledge of him who called us by his own glory and goodness'. (2 Peter 1:3). Why should we add additional things to it that are the products of our brain?

So much I have written about the Baptism rite is not to give up this ritual altogether but to differentiate between Biblical essential doctrines and manmade and custom-made rituals properly. Paul said 'That your faith should not stand in the wisdom of men, but in the power of God. Howbeit we speak wisdom among them that are perfect; yet not the wisdom of this world, nor of the princes of this world, that come to nought: But we speak the wisdom of God in a mystery, even the hidden wisdom, which God ordained before the world unto our glory:' (1Corinthians 2:5-7). We are supposed to be of the mind of Christ (v.16). I am not against baptism as far as it is used as a ritual for the initiation of a person or infant by aspersion affusion or immersion, as approved by that church, for membership. Making it the basic and fundamental faith element, according to my conviction, I emphasize, is not biblical. In any of the factors of our Christian faith, baptism in water is not essential mainly because it does not have any salvific effect. It is just a harmless practice if we practice it without linking it to our belief in Jesus Christ and the salvation by grace. Why should we put a piece of new garment upon an old, or new wine into old bottles? We are new creatures in Jesus Christ. We are the people of a new covenant bought with the precious and invaluable blood of Jesus. We are not expected to contaminate or defile the pure and blameless blood by which we are saved and made the citizens of the heavenly Kingdom. We are made the children of God and co-heirs with Jesus Christ by faith only.

Jesus once addressed the then generation and likened them with the children in the marketplace gaming in groups. They often complain that the others have not responded to their playing of the pipe or beat their breast in lamentation. It seems even now it is true. Among Christians they are forming groups who play according to their tunes and game planning. They are popularizing themselves with new ideologies and interpreting the words for own benefits. They change the rules of the game in their favor. In that generation also a large group of people were there who were bitter against Jesus because he was not living according to their interests. The message of repentance and of the Kingdom of God and the message of salvation was not acceptable to them. They criticized John saying he has a devil in him and Jesus saying he was gluttonous. The message of salvation is for all the time, and it is eternal. It cannot be changed, or no additions can be made to it. Now we see many new generation churches coming up with new tunes in their pipes and with new funeral melancholies. Those who do not approve of their practices and customs are condemned by them. As Jesus said, 'But wisdom is justified of her children'. (Matthew 11:16-19). The religious gamers of this generation make the whole Christian community despised and dishonored in the world around. What happens to our one God, one faith, one baptism theology? Do we accept the five *solae* formulated for the reformed Christian community as the doctrine of salvation?

My family's tradition as Christians hark back to the mid eighteenth century. My known parents of the last three generations were faithful to God to their last. They suffered a lot for the cause of faith physically and economically. Me too in my life is enjoying blessings immeasurable from the Lord my savior. My sufferings I count as blessings for my purification because I believe God so loves me. All my needs are met by him according to his time in his manner as he knows me better than I. His timeline is not that of mine, I understand. Our family's tradition was infant baptism. Our Lord has not denied his blessings and his amazing grace to us. I am greatly thankful to him and continue in a ministry by his grace appropriating the talents he has given me. Praising the Lord, I remain. Amen.